PICTORIAL HISTORY of KILMARNOCK

John Malkin

COVER:
Oil Paintings of old Kilmarnock
by Hugh Rankin

PICTORIAL HISTORY SERIES

uniform with this book

PICTORIAL HISTORY OF DUNDONALD
R. KIRK — ISBN 0-907526-39-X

PICTORIAL HISTORY OF GALSTON
J. MAIR — ISBN 0-907526-37-3

PICTORIAL HISTORY OF NEWMILNS
J. MAIR — ISBN 0-907526-34-9

forthcoming title:

PICTORIAL HISTORY OF DARVEL
J. MAIR — ISBN 0-907526-40-3

PICTORIAL HISTORY
of
KILMARNOCK

John Malkin

Alloway Publishing

© John Malkin, 1989

First Published in 1989
by Alloway Publishing Ltd.,
Darvel, Ayrshire

Printed in Scotland
by Walker & Connell Ltd.,
Hastings Square,
Darvel, Ayrshire.

ISBN No. 0-907526-42-X

BIBLIOGRAPHY

History of Kilmarnock, Archibald McKay; *Old Kilmarnock*, James Walker; *First, Second
and Third Statistical Accounts of Scotland*; *Kilmarnock Standard Files*; *Kilmarnock
Standard Annual Files*; *Kilmarnock Town Council Records and Publications*; *Ayrshire,
The Story Of A County*, John Strawhorn; *Ayrshire, A Social and Industrial Survey (1745-
1950)*, James Edward Shaw; *Retrospect Of An Artist's Life*, John Kelso Hunter; *Etchings
Of "Workers" Or Waning Crafts*, Robert Bryden; *Sketches Of Old Kilmarnock*, Thomas
Smelley; *The Boyds Of Kilmarnock*, Kilmarnock and Loudoun History Group;
Kilmarnock Equitable Co-operative Society, A Fifty-Year Record (1860-1910), William
Robertson; *History Of The Old High Kirk*, James Hunter; *Brass Tacks and A Fiddle*, A.V.
Christie; *Kilmarnock Football Club (1869-1969)*, Hugh Taylor; *Kilmarnock Cricket Club*,
James Aitchison; *Kilmarnock Rugby Club*, J.F.T. Thomson; *Curling: An Illustrated
History*, David B. Smith; *Green Cars To Hurlford*, Brian T. Deans; *Scottish Tramlines
(Kilmarnock Trams)*, Scottish Tramway Museum Society, *Contributions To Local
History*, David Landsborough.

INTRODUCTION

The history of Kilmarnock is a vast tapestry which records, for all who care to look, the development of this old, great, and radical Scottish town, from the magical, misty moments of unrecorded time to the graphic era we live in today. Woven by countless thousands, with the traditional skill of wabster chiels, the tapestry pulsates with the colour and movement of life itself.

In the fifty years I have been privileged to write about Kilmarnock, I have always been struck by the similarity between its history and the history of Scotland. Politically, industrially, socially, Kilmarnock is, and always has been, a microcosm of Scotland.

Subject matter for this book, therefore, has not been hard to find. Much harder has it been to make a selection which will do justice to the tapestry. What I have done, simply, is to highlight a few of the cameos woven into the warp and woof, the people who made the news and the events which have shaped the town.

As will be readily seen, this book is not an erudite work of history. Rather is it inspired by the writings of historians, spiced with the writings of story-tellers, chroniclers, songsters and poets of high or humble degree. Together, the selection means Kilmarnock to me, the town where I was born and which, by happy chance, has given me proud identity as one of its citizens.

While this book is unashamedly a very personal book, it is my hope that it will inspire readers, wherever they may live, to find out more about the magic of Kilmarnock.

As indicated by the bibliography, copy has been drawn from a wide area. I am indebted beyond measure to the writers. I am similarly indebted to all those who helped me by contributing photographs, supplying manuscripts and information, checking copy, and doing research. In this latter group, I include the staff of the Dick Institute Library and Museum; Miss Barbara Graham, Kilmarnock; Mr. Alex Marshall, Kilmarnock; Mr. Frank Beattie, Kilmarnock; Mr. David Richardson, Kilmarnock; Mr. Robert Kirk, Dundonald; Mr. R. Sime, Kilmarnock; Mr. J. Keachie, Kilmarnock; Mr. J. Stewart McLauchlan, Kilmarnock; George Outram & Co. Ltd., Glasgow; Riccarton History Group and the staff of Alloway Publishing.

I am also indebted to the Kilmarnock Standard for allowing Alloway Publishing to reprint a modified version of 'Burns in Auld Killie' written by myself and published in Kilmarnock Standard Annual 1958.

Kilmarnock
Ayrshire

John Malkin
1989

HISTORICAL SKETCH

IN THE BEGINNING

Many hundreds of years ago, when time was slipping by, still unrecorded by man, there was established at the confluence of two streams which we now call the Kilmarnock Water and the River Irvine a community, or settlement, which is now the town of Kilmarnock. That is about all that can be said with accuracy about the beginnings of Kilmarnock. As Descartes might have described things, Kilmarnock was because Kilmarnock is.

Fortunately for those privileged to be native to Kilmarnock, or those who have come here and established kinship, the mystery of origin has inspired much romantic speculation, and sometimes we come across a record which seems to support an opinion, or theory, with a little truth.

The popular view is that Kilmarnock developed from a Christian settlement set up, perhaps as early as the 4th or 5th century, by an Irish missionary called variously Marnoc or Mernoc, Marnock or Mernock, or Earnoch or Earnock. James Hunter, in *The Old High Kirk,* says that the name Kilmarnock is accepted by today's place-name experts to mean 'the church of beloved Earnock.'

"Confusingly," Mr. Hunter goes on, "a number of holy men of the early Church in Scotland and Ireland had this name, most of them living in the 7th, 8th and 9th centuries. It does not follow that any of these lived in, or preached in, or even visited, Kilmarnock, only that a church dedicated to one of them was later built there. Possibly, the dedication was because a relic of the Saint was gifted to the Church."

Along with others who have delved deeply into Kilmarnock's history, Mr. Hunter admits that it is impossible to say when the town began. "But", he says, "almost certainly, it stood exactly, or very close to, where the Laigh Kirk now stands. Certainly the mediaeval parish church of Kilmarnock stood on this spot."

While in agreement with Mr. Hunter about Kilmarnock's connection with an Irish saint, the *Second Statistical Account of Scotland* (1845) supports the popular belief that the 'Cell of Marnoc' was set up in the 4th century, not, as Mr. Hunter suggests, in the period from the 7th to the 9th century .

The compilers of the *Second Statistical Account* make no claim that Kilmarnock ever had any physical connection with a Marnock. On the contrary, they, too, think this unlikely. As evidence, they mention Kilmaronock

(Dunbartonshire) and Inch Marnock (Loch Lomond). Adding to the list, of course, there is Port Marnock in Ireland.

The 'saintly origin' theory is given powerful support in an article by Francis Croome published in the *Ordnance Gazeteer of Scotland* in 1883.

"The name, like that of the parish," says Mr. Croome, "is from Kil-marnoch, that is, the 'Church of St. Marnoch or Mernoch.' The word, Kilmarnock, is a contraction of Mo-ernin-occ, the prefix, (mo), meaning 'my' and the suffix, (occ), 'little.' The centre is the name of an Irish saint, Ernin or Ernene, who died about 634 AD, according to the *Annals of Ulster*."

It would seem, from Mr. Hunter and Mr. Croome, that Kilmarnock's saintly founder was, in fact, one of the monks who followed St. Columba (521-597) to Scotland and helped to establish Christianity there.

Mr. Croome adds to the 'saintly origin' theory an extraordinary anecdote about Ernin or Ernene.

"Adamnon, in his *Life of St. Columba,*" says Mr. Croome, "mentions Ernine as a boy, attached to the Monastery of Clonmaonoise, mean in dress and look... coming forward stealthily when St. Columba visited the Monastery that he might touch the hem of the cloak, which the blessed man wore, without his knowing."

Ernene's ploy was duly noticed by St. Columba who prophesied for him wisdom and prudence, good conduct and the virtues of the soul. "Great shall be Ernine's progress" said the Saint. "His tongue will receive the gift of God in wholesome doctrine and eloquence."

Adamnon backs St. Columba's prophecy by recording how Ernine became famous and honoured in all the churches in Ireland.

An alternative to the 'saintly origin' theory is offered by J. Kevan McDowall in *Carrick Gallovidian*. According to him, the Gaelic name for Kilmarnock is 'Cil-mor-cnoc,' literally, 'the hill (cil) of the great (mor) cairn (cnoc).'

Though it is impossible to identify the site referred to by Mr. McDowall, there is evidence to support his opinion. The area around Kilmarnock abounded at one time in prehistoric relics–mounds, tumuli, cairns, cists, urns and arrowheads.

No matter the reason why Kilmarnock is called Kilmarnock, here it stands today, a proud and venerable town, so very Scottish that its history has always been the radical history of Scotland. What the people of Kilmarnock have fought for, so the people of Scotland fought for. When Scotland suffered, so did Kilmarnock.

FROM ACORN TO OAK

Though of ancient origin, Kilmarnock managed to veil itself in secrecy until the early years of the 17th century.

Earliest descriptions of the town are at odds with each other. When Timothy Pont came here in 1609, he found "Kilmernock Toune a large village of great repair. It hath a fair stone bridge over the River Marnock. It hath a pretty church from vich the village Castell and Lordschipe takes its name."

Forty-six years later, along came Richard Franck from Cambridge on a fishing trip. If he is to be believed, Kilmarnock must have degenerated after Pont's visit.

Franck describes Kilmarnock as "an antient corporation, crowded with mechanics and brewhouses, a place, through the midst of whose crazy tottering ports, runs a river replenished with trout."

Franck speaks of Kilmarnock's "dirty streets and great rains which melt the muck and drive it into the River Marr." He goes on: "The inhabitants dwell in ugly houses, little better than huts, built so low that their eaves hang dangling to touch the earth. Not one good structure is to be found in Kilmarnock."

Despite his criticism of the physical appearance of Kilmarnock, Franck shows respect for the skills of its townspeople. "Part of their manufacture," he says, "is knitting of bonnets and weaving of Scottish cloth. For the temper of metals, they are without compeer. The men of Kilmarnock are particularly skilled in cutlery. They are artisans in dirks."

The description of Kilmarnock's houses in 1655 as ugly may be fairly accurate. It is possible they were built of basketwork frames filled in at the sides with turf coated in mud. Roofs were of brushwork, or turf, and windows were few.

Surrounded by lush farmland which suited sheep and cattle, blessed with the water of two rivers and plenty of coal to hand, the 17th-century inhabitants of Kilmarnock were skilled, not surprisingly, in the weaving of bonnets, cloth and stockings, and in the manufacture of high-grade steel for dirks and cutting instruments.

Though closely confined to the limits of their own living-space, the skills of Kilmarnock's inhabitants were deemed worthy of recognition by the superior, the fifth Lord Boyd. In 1591, Lord Boyd, through James VI, granted Kilmarnock a Charter empowering the inhabitants:

> to buy and sell wine, wax, cloth, woollens and linen, and other merchandise.
> to have in the burgh bakers, brewers, butchers, vendors of flesh and fish, and all other tradesmen belonging to a free Burgh of Barony.
> to have free burgesses, and, with the consent of Lord Boyd, elect bailies and officers for ruling the town.
> to have and hold a market cross and a market day weekly, and a free fair annually for eight days.

A home weaver at work.

This new status as a Burgh of Barony was exploited fully by Kilmarnock in the 18th century. Quickly, the town earned a high reputation for quality of manufacture and the consequent availability of work. People came into Kilmarnock from rural communities and nearby towns and villages. By the end of the century, population had increased to 8,000, over 1,200 more than it was 100 years earlier. To cope with increasing population, increasing manufacture, and increasing needs, Ayrshire authorities, helped by the Government, criss-crossed the County with excellent roads, giving communities ease of access to each other and linking them to the seaports of Troon, Irvine, Ayr and Ardrossan. John Loudon McAdam spent many years making roads in his native County before going south.

In 1811, Aiton had this to say of the Ayrshire road revolution: "There are probably few districts in Scotland where so many excellent roads have been made in so short a period." Traffic increased, farmers acquired carts, carriers set up in business to transport goods and produce to Glasgow and Edinburgh. Passenger traffic also increased; public coaches out-numbered private coaches on the roads. By the end of the 18th century, truly the century of the road' in Ayrshire, Kilmarnock, in addition to its many road connections inside the County, was a recognised stop on the daily coach run from Glasgow to Dumfries and Carlisle. Later, the town became a stop on the mail-coach run over the same route. The trade generated by the coach runs was responsible immediately for improvement in the route through the Cross.

By the 1770s, Kilmarnock had become one of the principal manufacturing towns in Scotland. Local wool had to be supplemented by stocks brought in from other parts of Scotland. Products of the weaving and spinning industry included linen, blankets, serges, shalloons, duffles and stockings. Blankets were acknowledged to be 'equal to those manufactured in England.'

Tanning, dressing and currying of leather increased, leading to extension of Kilmarnock's shoe trade. Goods were transported to Greenock by road and thence by sea to foreign countries.

Important new trades were added before the end of the 18th century—calico printing, worsted shawl printing, and carpet-making. All were to add to Kilmarnock's prosperity.

Carpet-making is still one of Kilmarnock's most important industries. It was introduced about 1728 by Mrs. Maria Gardiner (great aunt of Lord Kilmarnock). An admirer of what she called 'useful arts,' Mrs. Gardiner brought spinners and weavers from Dalkeith to Kilmarnock. Under her guidance, Kilmarnock spinners and wabsters improved the art of carpet-making and made it a considerable source of wealth to Kilmarnock.

By 1800, Kilmarnock had some 200 looms in production. One thousand adults, and about 800 boys and girls, were employed. In addition, the town had work for calico printers, cutlers, tanners, dressers, skinners, and curriers.

If the 18th century is correctly seen as the century of the road, then the 19th century has to be the century of the railway. The Iron Horse was to be an even greater stimulus to trade than the old cart or wagon horse. Nowhere is the change seen to greater effect than on the Kilmarnock-to-Troon Railway built by the Duke of Portland in 1808 to take coal from Kilmarnock to the coast. This, the first railway in Scotland, ran for almost ten miles to Troon by way of a bridge over the River Irvine and through Shewalton Moss. Wagon-loads weighing 12 tons were hauled by horses. In 1816, a Stephenson steam locomotive was tried on the railway. Maximum weight pulled by the Iron Horse proved to be no more than 10 tons–and at only 5 mph.

Besides being Scotland's first railway, the Duke of Portland's tram-road was also the first to carry passengers. During the summer holidays, the coal wagons carried Kilmarnock weavers to Barassie. Their 'superiors' travelled in a special coach like a gipsy caravan. At its height, the railway and its horses transported 200,000 tons of goods and provisions a year.

Kilmarnock's rail links increased rapidly in the 19th century. In 1837, the Kilmarnock/Ayr Railway Company was formed. Six years later, the Glasgow/Dalry railway reached Kilmarnock and was soon carrying goods and passengers. The old Kilmarnock/Troon line was bought from the Duke of Portland, adapted and re-opened for steam trains in 1847. That same year (1847), the Kilmarnock/Irvine line was opened. By 1850, it had been extended to Galston and Newmilns; and, by 1895, to Darvel. After three years in construction, the Glasgow and South Western Railway's Nithsdale line between Glasgow and Carlisle was opened in 1850. Kilmarnock was one of the points of call.

By the middle of the 19th century, Kilmarnock had been linked by rail with Glasgow via Stewarton, and had seen the Glasgow and South Western Railway open a workshop and locomotive-building shop at Bonnyton, Kilmarnock. Almost 18,000,000 passengers had been carried by rail when the century closed.

The extensive road and rail network created in Ayrshire (and throughout lowland Scotland) in little more than a year confirmed Kilmarnock's supremacy as a manufacturing, commercial and agricultural centre.

Information presented before a Committee of the House of Lords in 1846 graphically illustrates the huge volume of trade passing between Kilmarnock and England. Into Kilmarnock came drapery, ironmongery, sugar, leather and trimmings for footwear, seeds, printwork materials, tea and porter. Out to England, to London, went seeds, leather and skins, carpets, and military and other bonnets. It was fortunate for Kilmarnock that it had many other markets to offset its balance-of-trade deficit with England.

With the disastrous flood of 1852 in mind, caused by better land drainage the experts said (see Water, Water Everywhere), it is interesting to note that the Duke of Portland, in 1825 and 1826, imported over 60,000,000 drain tiles from England, and brought in another 1,000,000 from other sources.

Decline in products of the tanneries, hand-loom weaving, and calico-printing began to show towards the end of the 19th century. By 1909, the only surviving printfield in the town was employing its workforce cutting blocks, not for worsted shawls or calico, but for lino and other floor coverings made in England. The craft of hand shoe-making was also virtually gone. In its place, in 1873, A.L. Clark & Company (established 1820) had set up a steam-power footwear factory. The Company was later to change its name to the Saxone Shoe Company and establish a world-wide respect for footwear bearing the name Saxone.

Various ingenious inventions by Thomas Morton, a local mechanic, helped the carpet industry to survive and compete successfully with foreign as well as UK competition. (see TOWER, OBSERVATORY AND CASTLE). Carpet firms declined in number, however, and, as the 20th century was beginning, only one remained–Robert Blackwood & Sons, Burnside, forerunner of the present BMK, still a powerful force today in the industry.

With confidence born of success, Kilmarnock opened a new door for every one which closed. Introduction of the power loom to the Irvine Valley in 1879 was quickly followed by its arrival in Kilmarnock. In 1880, John Fleming & Company had 15 power looms producing lace curtains in their Belford Mills. Some thirty years on (1909), Nottingham lace and madras curtains were added to Kilmarnock's textiles trade.

Wool-spinning, cotton-fabric and woollen-fabric manufacture were all reliable sources of employment and wealth in the early years of the present century. Hundreds of weavers and spinners were engaged in preparing wool for weaving into carpets, tweeds, blankets, costume-length cloth, shirtings, winceys, blouse materials, colonial flannels. One firm was specialising in weaving white cottons for India and China. Another turned out knitted goods for wholesale.

The 19th century, of course, is remembered in Kilmarnock for one product more than any other. In 1820, John Walker established a whisky-blending business which was to become the principal business of its kind in the world. For 170 years, Johnnie Walker, now part of the Guinness empire, has been the world's favourite whisky, and has given seven generations of Kilmarnock people steady employment.

Kilmarnock it was that gave the world 'Real Mackay' whisky and, with it, a colourful synonym for 'the real thing'. Taking over the whisky firm of William Wallace & Company, Mr. David Mackay, then Provost of Kilmarnock, developed it so successfully that in tribute, the firm named its whisky 'The Real Mackay.'

Not far behind Johnnie Walker as an advertisement for Kilmarnock abroad is the hydraulic-engineering firm of Glenfield and Kennedy Limited. Formed in 1899 from The Kennedy Patent Water Meter Company (1852) and The Glenfield Iron Company (1865), Glenfield and Kennedy has always been a prime employer of labour in Kilmarnock. It has survived receivership, two takeovers by U.S. companies, and is now in business as Biwater Valves Ltd. Glenfield water-control equipment is in use all over the world.

Increasing the diversity of Kilmarnock's industry, Andrew Barclay & Company began building locomotives in 1840. Much the same activity was introduced in 1859 by the Glasgow & South Western Railway. In 1859, Grant Ritchie & Company Limited started in engineering at Townholm and, in 1885, Dick, Kerr & Company Limited began building colliery, tram and railway plant at Britannia Works. Tiles, sanitary ware, bricks and faience were introduced by Southhook Pottery at Bonnyton and Shanks & Company at Longpark.

Kilmarnock's rapid progress as a manufacturing town (the Glasgow of Ayrshire it was now being called) is nowhere more evident than in census returns. These show that, from 1801 to 1901, Kilmarnock's population increased from 8,079 to 34,165. To cope with the changes, Kilmarnock had to invoke the Charter of 1691 by encouraging the introduction of service businesses– furniture shops, joiners, plumbers, newspapers, aerated waters, chemists, printing, newsagents, bookshops, gunsmiths, ironmongers, clothing, builders, etc.

To meet the demand for more living and working space, the town crept quietly but quickly away from its over-crowded centre. By 1800, New Street, Waterloo Street, Green Street, and East Shaw Street had given the town a little elbow room. The town bridge had been improved and Townhead Bridge built. In 1805, King Street was formed, taking coach traffic off narrow Sandbed. Between 1812 and 1830, Portland Street, East Shaw Street and West Shaw Street were in use. Duke Street was opened in 1859, and an extension made to Bentinck Street in 1872.

The present century began in Kilmarnock with the ill-fated introduction of tramcars by the Town Council in 1904. They were never seen on the roads again after the end of the 1926 General Strike. The Corporation electric power station, built to supply the trams with power, survived.

Not much addition was made to industry between the end of the Great War in 1918 and the start of the 1939-45 war. The 'regulars' held on–Glenfield, Walkers, BMK, Barclays, Saxone, Barr Thomson, etc. Southhook,

Shanks, Glasgow & South Western Railway workshops, Grant Ritchie, Britannia Works have now closed down. Glacier Metal came along in 1948 to make plain bearings for the automotive industry at their Kirkstyle Factory and are still in business. Unfortunately, Massey-Ferguson closed their combine-harvester plant at Moorfield in the early 1980s after 30 years.

According to the Industrial Index compiled by Kilmarnock Venture, something like 170-180 firms are operating in Kilmarnock today. Forty-five of these are to be found in the eight or nine small industrial estates which have been established by local authority and Government. Most of them are engaged in traditional manufacture, but one or two are looking to more modern products. Proven Engineering, Moorfield, for instance, specialise in micro-computer applications, robotics, and wind turbines. Detection Instruments (Northern) Limited, Bonnyton, manufacture fire and gas detection and protection systems for marine and off-shore application.

A breakdown of the 45 firms which have taken root in the industrial estates shows that 23 employ up to 10 workers, 9 up to 25, 4 up to 50, 6 up to 100, and 2 up to 150. Is it from these that the new Glenfields, Walkers, Barclays, BMKs, and Barr Thomsons will come?

A typical Scottish pithead round about 1900.

9

THE COST OF COAL

The pithead scene on the previous page prompts memory of four fatal pit accidents which occurred in Kilmarnock in the first quarter of the present century.

In July 1900, an explosion in a Portland Coal Company pit, The Nursery, claimed the lives of three colliers and brought injury to another five. Another explosion in the same pit in February, 1908, killed four colliers.

Kirkstyle, another Portland Coal Company pit, was the scene of a third fatal explosion on 18th January, 1925. On that day, five colliers, including a father and his 15-year-old son, were killed. The tragedy was marked by a memorial service in Hurlford Parish Church.

Worst of the four Kilmarnock pit accidents occurred in December, 1909, at Caprington No. 41 (The Mains), owned by Caprington and Auchlochan Coal Company Limited. Subsidence of an old working caused water from the River Irvine to flood The Mains. Ten of the 16 workers in the pit at the time were drowned, two of them boys. The other six survived.

GOLDBERRY HILL AND THE BOYDS

There doesn't seem much doubt that the words 'Gold Berry,' which appear in the Coat of Arms of the Boyds of Kilmarnock, identify a hill where a crucial engagement in the Battle of Largs was fought in 1263.

According to the *History of Rowallane,* Acho or Haakon, King of Norway, "landit at Air with 160 schips and 20,000 men" to claim land promised by Macbeth to his predecessors but not yet handed over. The Rowallan account identified Arran, Bute and the two Cumbraes as the land claimed by Haakon.

The Norwegians were heavily defeated by the Scots under Alexander the Third. But, where did the Sir Robert Boyd come from, who, along with a company of soldiers, put the Norwegians to flight at Goldberry Hill, south of the main engagement.

The popular story in the annals of Kilmarnock is that Sir Robert was in possession of Dean Castle when the Norwegians landed, and that it was a band of his tenants he marched the 30 miles to Largs to help his King. Yet, according to Fullarton, quoted in McKay's *History of Kilmarnock,* the first reliable reference to the Boyd family was as "vassals of the De Morvilles in the Regality of Largs."

It is possible that Sir Robert Boyd, victor at Goldberry Hill, was living, not at Kilmarnock, but at Largs, when the battle took place. This could well have been the case, as McKay himself bears witness. After Goldberry Hill, McKay tells us, Sir Robert was rewarded by Alexander the Third with grants of several lands in Cunningham.

Whether the Boyds were in possession of the lands and Castle of Dean before 1263, or came by them afterwards as reward from Alexander, is never likely to be known. They were certainly in the neighbourhood of Kilmarnock in the last few years of the 13th century, joining other Scot-

tish nobles under Wallace in the fight to drive the English from Scotland.

The Boyd family coat of arms.

HAMMER OF THE ENGLISH

A few facts, an abundance of legend, but, above all, an unashamed indulgence in wishful thinking have combined to create in the receptive Kilmarnock mind the belief that the Scottish freedom fighter, Sir William Wallace, was truly born in Kilmarnock. We really believe in Kilmarnock that, when Sir William was dubbed the 'Knight of Ellerslie', those who conferred the title upon him were locating him in Ellerslie, Riccarton.

Claims, of course, can also be made that Wallace's birthplace was Elderslie in Renfrewshire. In the days when Wallace was battling with the English invaders, many Wallace families were to be found in Renfrewshire. Some had actually left the Kilmarnock area to live there.

The Renfrewshire association with Wallace is easy to understand, yet there is ample evidence in fact, and in legend, to show that the Patriot, Regent of Scotland, Victor of Stirling Bridge, 'Hammer of the English' was born in Riccarton in the year 1270, perhaps in Riccarton Castle where we know his father was born.

Where the Wallace Castle of Riccarton stood used to be marked by a plaque. The plaque has been removed because of redevelopment: it will be returned to Riccarton in good time. Only a few miles away stand the ruins of Craigie Castle, long the residence of the Ayrshire Wallaces who held sway over the lands of Riccarton.

The view that Wallace was, in fact, a Riccarton man, born and bred, was the reason why, after the Great War of 1914-1918, some Riccarton inhabitants formed the Wallace Club.

According to the *Third Statistical Account of Scotland* (1951), Riccarton is thought to take its name from Wallace's uncle Richard. Richardtoon could so easily become Riccarton.

"Under the leadership of Baillie James Burnett," says the Account "the Riccarton Wallace Club studied the various places in the parish associated with the Wallace family, and erected a plaque in the house (reference to Riccarton Castle) in Fleming Street where Wallace was born."

The *Third Statistical Account* notes that one of the exploits which the Wallace Club kept fresh was his fight with an English occupying force on the banks of the *Erewynn Water,* (River Irvine).

Archibald Adamson, a local chronicler, takes up the tale:

> A little below the water meetings (confluence of the Kilmarnock Water and the River Irvine) stands the farmhouse of Maxholm. Near to it, a thorn tree called the 'Bickering Bush' stood, marking the spot where Wallace was set upon by English soldiers while fishing.
>
> A troop happening to ride past, five of them demanded the fish Wallace had taken...an altercation ensued...one dismounted to help himself to the fish. Wallace struck the soldier down with his fishing rod, wrenched his sword from him, and, with a back stroke, cut off the fellow's head. Seeing the fate of their comrade, the others dismounted to avenge his death; two of them met a similar fate.

Following this bloody encounter, Wallace made for Riccarton Castle to tell what had happened. Suspecting the English would be bent on vengeance, the housekeeper persuaded Wallace to don a mutch and gown and sit at a spinning wheel. Wallace had just begun spinning when the avengers appeared, demanding to know if the killer of their comrades was there. "Search the place," the housekeeper said. That they did but found nothing more suspicious than a spinning lass.

Riccarton Wallace Club is no longer in existence, but somewhere there might be a snuff box with a strong flavour of Wallace about it. According to David Landsborough in *Contributions to Local History,* published 1879, there was then, in the possession of a Mr. James Paxton, a snuff box made from the wood of the 'Bickering Bush.' The inscription on the box commemorated Wallace's defeat of five of Lord Percy's retainers.

Adamson strengthens the Wallace-Riccarton connection by describing his visit to Barnweil Hill where, according to legend, Wallace paused to look back upon the

barns of Ayr, which he had set alight to revenge the murder by the English of his uncle and other nobles.

The Barnweil Monument.

"As the flames shot Heavenward," said Mr. Adamson, "Wallace exclaimed, 'The barns of Ayr burn weil.'"

On top of Barnweil Hill stands a castellated tower, 80 feet high, erected in memory of Wallace in 1858. Tablets on three sides pay verbose, but none the less merited, tribute to "the nation's greatest hero, victor of Stirling Bridge, who threw off the yoke of foreign oppression, and maintained the independence and nationality of Scotland."

Mr. Adamson, with some justification, finds the monument and lavish verbal tributes akin to an affront to Wallace. "Had Wallace fought for Greece of old," he says, "his countrymen would have preserved his ashes in a golden urn, and hewn his monument from a mountain. Never would they have allowed centuries to lapse before they raised a stone to his memory."

"Stone, lime and tall talk make a poor monument to a national benefactor. The memory of the great and good is best preserved when enshrined in the hearts of their countrymen, when their names and deeds are handed down from generation to generation by an appreciative people."

11

Mr. Adamson makes a very valid point. But is recognition of a man's unselfish sacrifice and endeavours any less worthy because it is belated? We do well to remember that Kilmarnock, in 1858, was still suffering from the punishment and privation many of its citizens had suffered a few decades before in their fight for better social conditions through fairer representation in Parliament.

The Barnweil Monument could be seen as a symbol linking the 13th-century Scottish patriot with his 19th-century fellow Scots.

Wallace's contribution to eventual defeat of the English at Bannockburn in 1314 was massive. His own victory at Stirling Bridge indicated some above-average skill in generalship, but it was as a guerilla leader that he excelled. The English had reason to fear Wallace more, perhaps, than any other Scottish freedom fighter. His execution after capture was inevitable and barbaric.

A TALE OF MYSTERY AND IMAGINATION

Like it or lump it, Kilmarnock is stuck with Lord Soulis. Many centuries ago, some say the 15th, some the 14th, others locate it as 'Once upon a time,' there was erected in the middle of a cobbled street in Kilmarnock a monolith of grey sandstone, topped with a cross. Local inhabitants dubbed the monolith the 'Soulis Cross' in memory of an English adventurer of that name who had been bested in a fight with one of the Boyds of Dean Castle.

Though Timothy Pont, the topographer, dated the Soulis Cross as 1444 when he visited Kilmarnock in 1609, it is more than likely, that he was doing no better than guess.

If the date 1444, said to have been on the original Soulis Cross, is correct, then the Cross could not have been meant as a monument to any Lord Soulis.

Soulis Cross.

Holding full power over the Lowlands of Scotland between 1292 and Bannockburn in 1314, Edward I was free to send a favourite, Sir John de Soulis, to Scotland in the 1290s armed with 'letters of attorney' which suggest his purpose was to help in the subjugation of the Scots. Bannockburn ended Edward's plan in 1314, and the Soulises, every one of them, were back in England by 1320, regretting, as they had every right to do, that they had ever left.

So, if a Lord Soulis *did* perish at the hands of a Boyd, it had to be before 1320. Round about that year, King Robert the Bruce conferred upon Lord Robert Boyd the lands of Kilmarnock, Bonnyton and Hareshaw in gratitude for his support in the defeat of the English.

Dubbing the original Cross as 'The Soulis' led at once to naming the street where it first stood as Soulis Street. There it stood until 1825 when, because of the danger it was posing for horse-drawn carts, carriages, stage coaches and mail coaches, it was lifted and set down in the Old High Kirk Yard nearby.

The Soulis story was not allowed to rest there. In the very year of removal of the Cross from Soulis Street, a fluted column was unveiled in a niche set into the wall of the Old High Kirk. The inscription read:

To the memory of Lord Soulis, 1444.
Erected by subscription 1825.
'The days of old to mind I call.'

No reason given for the tribute. No hint of what Lord Soulis had done to merit a monument.

Today, the original Soulis Cross is in its third home, the Dick Institute Museum.

Who, then, was the Lord Soulis, believed to have been killed by Lord Robert Boyd with a crossbow somewhere on the banks of Kilmarnock Water? No matter his identity, certain it is that Lord Soulis, subject of Kilmarnock's only ancient monument, has stuck to Kilmarnock like a familiar spirit, a benevolent one, for centuries.

COVENANTING KILMARNOCK

The militant support which the Covenanters were given in Kilmarnock helped to ensure, against harassment, persecution and intimidation, the survival of Presbyterianism as the established religion of Scotland.

James the Sixth's fondness for Episcopalianism, even before he accepted the throne of England in 1603, was viewed with nothing short of suspicion by the Scottish people. When his son, Charles I, showed continued support for Episcopalianism on accession to the throne in 1625, the Scots put a shot across his bows by swearing under covenant to uphold Presbyterianism in Scotland. In 1638, the Scots in great number signed the National Covenant, some in their own blood. Five years later, in 1643, the Solemn League and Covenant was drawn up.

Persecution of the Covenanters took violent form in the reign of Charles II. Adherence to the Covenants became unacceptable to authority. Covenanters were driven underground, forced to hold services behind closed doors, or out on the moors where the flatness of the terrain protected them against surprise attack by the soldiery. Weapons were hidden, ready for use if needed.

Kilmarnock showed its allegiance to the Covenants soon after the Persecution began. In 1666, the heads of John Ross and John Shields, Ayrshire Covenanters, executed in Edinburgh, were set up at Kilmarnock as a warning to the populace. In dead of night, the heads were taken down and secretly buried. They lie today, with other victims of the Persecution, in the graveyard of the Laigh Kirk.

Defeat of the Covenanters at Pentland in 1667 was followed by occupation of Kilmarnock by General Dalziel and his soldiers. 'Bloody Dalziel' extorted money, sanctioned torture, and packed the Tolbooth with so many prisoners that they could not lie or sit down. One man who did not have the information Dalziel wanted was shot out of hand. What part, if any, the Earl of Kilmarnock took in the cruelty is not known, but it is known that his residence, Dean Castle, was used as quarters for Dalziel's soldiers.

The year after Dalziel left (1678), Kilmarnock was invaded by a force of Government Highlanders. Once again, the town was plundered, ransacked and pillaged.

As part of the campaign to suppress Kilmarnock's sympathies for the Covenanters, one of them, John Finlay, was executed in Edinburgh. The crime does not seem to have made Kilmarnock conform. In 1683, "in order that the inhabitants and those in the neighbourhood, might be cowed into submission by the fearful spectacle," John Nisbet of Loudoun was publicly hanged at The Cross. His body lies in the Laigh Kirkyard. Both Finlay and Nisbet were condemned to death for the 'crime' of fighting with the Covenanters at Bothwell Bridge.

Another act of cruelty and oppression arising from Bothwell Bridge took place in 1679. Transportation for life was the sentence passed at Edinburgh upon 257 Covenanters, among them six men of Kilmarnock. During the voyage from Leith, the ship foundered on rocks near the Orkneys with great loss of life. Only one of the Kilmarnock six survived–Patrick Watt. In the Laigh Kirkyard is a memorial to the others–Thomas Finlay, John Cuthbertson, William Brown, and Robert and James Anderson.

Persecution of the Covenanters was over, and Scotland's established religion secured, when the Scottish Stuart Dynasty ended with the exile of Catholic James II in 1688 and the succession of Protestant William of Orange to the throne of the United Kingdom.

HIS OWN EXECUTIONER

A penchant for making wrong decisions, aggravated by circumstances and weaknesses beyond his control, created in William Boyd, 4th Earl of Kilmarnock, a force which destroyed him as surely as the Delphic Oracle destroyed Oedipus.

From the moment he succeeded to the title on the death of his father in 1715, events enticed him unerringly to his death on the scaffold at the age of 41.

Son of William, the 3rd Earl, and Euphemia, daughter of Lord Rosse of Hawkhead, near Paisley, the 4th Earl was born into a family of staunch Presbyterian faith and equally-staunch Hanoverian and Union sympathies.

An irresistible love of the good life led the Earl into extravagant spending and consequent neglect of his Kilmarnock estates. Pleasant in disposition and in looks, he spent much of his time in riding, fencing, dancing, music, travel abroad, interests which he seemed to regard as not improper for someone of his station.

The Earl's courtship and marriage in 1724, happy though it was most of the time, kept him on course for downfall. He was only 19 when he began to court 15-year-old Ann Livingston of Callendar and Livingston. The Dowager Lady Livingston's disapproval of the match was not confined to her awareness of the Earl's shortage of money. The Livingstons were Episcopalians and Jacobites. Only a year earlier (1723), her husband had died in Rome, exiled there, his estates forfeited, because of his support for the Jacobites in the '15 Rebellion.

With no better than unwilling consent from the Dowager, the Earl married Ann. By the time he had come of age, he was the father of two sons.

Responsibilities of parenthood were added to at once. A habitual gambler, Lady Euphemia, the Earl's mother, was incapable of prudent management of her affairs. Legal action against her for payment of gambling debts caused embarrassment to her family. Some alleviation of the financial drain upon family resources seemed in prospect when Lady Euphemia married Mr. John Murray. The opposite was the case. The marriage ran into immediate trouble, and Mr. Murray was forced to take legal action preventing his wife from running up debts in his name. Lady Euphemia died in 1729, only two years after her second marriage.

The Earl and Countess divided their time between Kilmarnock House, home of the Boyds since fire destroyed Dean Castle in 1735, and Callendar House, Falkirk. The Earl was specially keen to live at Callendar House. Here, in comfortable surroundings, he was able to find a little relaxation. Falkirk was more tolerant of Jacobite Episcopalians than was Presbyterian, Covenanting Kilmarnock.

Shortage of cash became more and more acute, and sometimes reached a stage when the Earl was quite unable even to meet food bills. Education for his family had to be paid for, repairs and improvements to the mansions in Kilmarnock and Falkirk, increased entertainment on a scale befitting social position had to be provided, gambling debts incurred in less responsible years would not go away.

Political involvement at national level required much effort from the Earl. An offer to help in the election of Sir Robert Walpole earned him a pension of £400. Failure of the campaign put an end to this source of a cash. Two payments totalling £300 was all he was given out of the Privy Purse. In Kilmarnock, the Earl found no friends among politicians. Indeed, when, on one occasion, he delegated to Lady Ann the duty of selecting bailies from a Council list, the Council declared its right to question the validity of any future arrangement of this kind.

One way out of trouble for the Earl might have been in stepping up production on his land. Since this kind of work did not appeal to him, he gave it no serious thought. He was interested in industry and commerce, but financial constraints prevented him from sinking capital in the town's increasing production of manufactured goods. Turning again off the right road, the Earl lost what capital he could spare in an abortive coal-mining adventure.

The Earl's final mistake was his greatest. He happened to be in Callendar House in September 1745 when there arrived none other than Prince Charles Edward Stuart, the Pretender. He was on the march from the west coast of Scotland, where he had landed, to Edinburgh in the hope of winning back the throne of Britain for the Stuarts.

Both Prince and Earl being similarly pleasant in disposition, a friendly relationship quickly established itself. Victory for the Jacobites at Prestonpans strengthened the Earl's approval of the Prince. Weighed down by debt, prospects drear, he began to see the Prince and the Jacobite cause as his salvation. His Presbyterianism proved no discouragement, in the circumstances, to the feeling that was coming over him–that he could espouse the Jacobite cause. He convinced himself that the Prince could not possibly be the kind of ruler who would sell out to Rome.

In spite of warnings from Lady Ann, reminders of what happened to her father and her family for supporting the '15 Jacobite Rebellion, the Earl threw his lot in with the Prince. It was, he told his wife, the wisest decision he had ever made.

Circumstances were soon to prove how strong was the Earl's penchant for adopting lost causes. His two sons were divided in allegiance as were their parents. Charles joined his father in support of the Jacobite cause but James remained loyal to the pro-Hanoverian Government.

Though the Earl was a member of the Prince's inner council, and privy to the planning of strategy, he was never advanced to first-line duties. He took the surrender of Carlisle Castle on the march into England, but unfavourable public reaction to the Prince and his ambitions slowly caused him to doubt the military wisdom of invading Eng-land. Retreat from Derby was a military necessity which, thanks to the generalship of Lord George Murray, was achieved in good order.

Meeting up with another Jacobite force near Bannockburn, the Jacobite army managed to defeat a Government force at Falkirk and take 300 prisoners. But the end was in sight. Retreating northwards towards Inverness, tired, ill-clad and ill-equipped, dispirited, short of horses, the Prince's army was routed at Culloden by the Duke of Cumberland's soldiers.

As the Prince and his army fled the field, the Earl of Kilmarnock made towards what he thought was a troop of fellow Jacobites. When he realised it was a Government troop, the Earl said he was 'surrendering to the mercy of the King.' His ruse was to do him no good, and, before he died, he admitted that he had made a mistake of identity. His surrender was made all the more ignominious because it was witnessed by his son, James.

Last act of a tragic life was played out in the Painted Chamber, Westminster, on 28th July 1746.

The Earl of Kilmarnock and Lord Balmerino were sentenced to death for high treason. Petitions and pleas for mercy, one of them from the people of Kilmarnock, were many. They had no effect. The Duke of Cumberland's report to the King that rumour credited the Earl of Kilmarnock with endorsing orders from Lord George Murray to kill all prisoners taken at Culloden, was taken as truth. No such orders were ever given, but execution orders for Kilmarnock and Balmerino were signed and carried out on Tower Hill on 18th August 1746.

THE EFFIGIES
of the late
EARL of KILMARNOCK, and the late LORD BALMERINO

After the execution of her husband, Lady Kilmarnock sought consolation in walking alone along the Kilmarnock Water from her home, Kilmarnock House.

In the time of the Boyds, the Kilmarnock hugged the line of the Walk as it is today. So far from finding consolation, the Countess found only distress. She retired from the world, and died in September 1747, a year after her husband, in her 39th year.

An old print shows Countess Ann setting out from Kilmarnock House.

Ashton Carle, a minstrel of the day, tells the tragic story of Countess Ann:

A wild, weird look has the Lady's Walk,
    And the trees are stripp'd and old;
They solemn bend in mute-like talk,
    In the twilight grey and cold.

Each gaunt and rugged sinewy root,
    Starts up along the way–
Memento sad of the lady's foot
    That erst did mournful stray.

Ghost-like the boughs loom in the sky,
    And, skeleton-like, they meet;
The very pathway, white and dry,
    Curves like a winding-sheet.

The rustling leaves that Autumn weaves
    In wither'd hillocks lie,
And the chilly wind soughs just behind
    Like the lady's tearful sigh.

Heavily rolls the evening mist,
    And the rising night winds throb,
By root and shoot, just where they list,
    Till they sound like the lady's sob.

Then this is the far-fam'd Lady's Walk,
    And walketh she there tonight?
Holdeth her spirit silent talk
    With that moon so sickly white?

Nothing gives Kilmarnock people greater pride than the knowledge that Robert Burns had the highest regard for the town. In its neuks and streets, its houses and taverns, Burns spent some of his happiest times. Repeatedly, he records his affection in poetry and correspondence. The 'special relationship' is also acknowledged in the fact that Kilmarnock is the home of the worldwide Burns Federation.

Here, in Kilmarnock, in John Wilson's printing house in the Star Inn Close off Waterloo Street, the first edition of the poet's works was printed. It is known of the worthy printer that he was a man of unimpeachable character and great piety, so it is difficult, therefore, to accept the popular belief that he was the hero of the poet's malicious *Epitaph On Wee 'Johnie'*, (The Complete Works Of Robert Burns, page 71):

Whoe'er thou art, O reader, know
That Death has murder'd Johnie,
An' here his *body* lies fu' low;
For saul he ne'er had onie.

It is true the poet was not too taken by Mr. Wilson's statement of expenses in connection with printing the Kilmarnock Edition, and that he resented Mr. Wilson's refusal to print a second edition, but he was known to have a high regard for the printer and is unlikely, therefore, to have had him in mind when he wrote the epitaph. A more likely story is the one which links 'Wee Johnie' with a certain Reverend gentleman from the neighbourhood of Ochiltree.

Another of Burns's epitaphs, the one to Robert Muir, recalls a Kilmarnock acquaintance whose friendship was very dear to his heart. It was in the home of Tam Samson on Tanker Ha' Brae that the poet met Mr. Muir, the company often including, besides Mr. Samson and Mr. Muir, such friends of the poet as Goldie, Parker and Gavin Turnbull.

It was Mr. Muir the poet consulted before making final arrangements for publishing his Kilmarnock edition. Mr. Muir ordered 70 copies of the edition and also 60 copies of the subsequent Edinburgh edition. Very little is known of the personal history of this good man except that he was a wine merchant whose premises were situated in the neighbourhood of Regent Street. He died in 1788, and the poet expressed his sorrow in *Epitaph on Robert Muir* (The Complete Works Of Robert Burns, page 322):

What man could esteem, or what woman could love,
    Was he who lies under this sod:
If such Thou refusest admission above,
    Then whom wilt Thou favour, Good God?

The remains of Tam Samson, and of Dr. Mackinlay and Rev. Mr. Robertson, who were given a certain notoriety by the poet in verse, lie in the Laigh Kirkyard. John Wilson lies in the Old High Churchyard.

Tam Samson, immortalised in the famous *Elegy on Tam Samson*, (The Complete Works Of Robert Burns, page 239), was one of Burns's most respected friends. Mr. Samson's house was a favourite howf of the poet on his frequent visits to Kilmarnock.

John Wilson's Printing House.

Yet another favourite ca' house for Burns was Sandy Paitrick's Tavern at the head of the Foregate. A son-in-law of the redoubtable Mr. Samson, Sandy Paitrick was famous locally for the quality of his wines and especially for his home-brewed ale.

Mackinlay and Robertson, immortalised in the famous Elegy and again in *The Ordination*, (The Complete Works Of Robert Burns, page 192), illustrate Burns's vehement dislike of the orthodoxy of the Kirk. The story goes that, in 1764, when Burns was only five years old, the then Earl of Glencairn, exercising his rights of patronage, installed the Rev. William Lindsay, a Moderate, or 'New Light,' minister in the pastorate of the High Kirk.

There was immediate uproar from the congregation but Mr. Lindsay remained in the charge until he died in 1774. Though succeeded by another 'New Light' minister, Rev. John Mutrie, the reign of the Moderates was near an end. When Mr. Mutrie died, the then Lord Glencairn surrendered to the Orthodox or 'Auld Light' group and appointed the Rev. Dr. James Mackinlay to the charge. In

The Ordination, Burns takes up the cudgels on behalf of the 'New Lights,' and belabours and ridicules the Calvanistic hypocrisy of Mackinlay, Robertson and their supporters.

Being a Mason, Burns was wont to foregather with his brethren when in Kilmarnock, and the Lodge which received his patronage was St. John's No. 22 which met in Croft Street. An honorary member of the Lodge, Burns had a high esteem for his fellow masons, especially Major William Parker, of Assloss House, their Right Worshipful Master. He mentions the Lodge and Major Parker in his *Masonic Song*, (The Complete Works Of Robert Burns, page 255). The last four lines of the poem are worth quoting as typifying the Masonic creed:

Within this dear mansion, may wayward Contention
    Or witherèd Envy ne'er enter!
May secrecy round be the mystical bound,
    And brotherly Love be the centre!

Another Mr. Parker, Christian name Hugh, was frequently visited by Burns in Kilmarnock. He is the inspiration of *Epistle to Hugh Parker*, (The Complete Works Of Robert Burns, page 322). Little is known of Mr. Parker, not even his place of abode in the town.

Two others whom the Bard was pleased to number among his Kilmarnock friends were Bailie Greenshields, a brewer from Grange Street, and Gavin Turnbull, an actor-cum-poet, who met with more appreciation from Burns himself than from the public.

Then there was John Goldie, ('Goudie, terror o' the Whigs,') a man of strong character, who lived and worked in a building off the Cross; tradition has it that it was here the poet corrected the proofs of his First Edition.

Tam Samson's House.

16

A TALE OF TWO CHURCHES

Early last century, considerable loss of life and injury was caused when the congregations in two Kilmarnock churches, the Laigh and St. Marnock's, were stampeded into a rush for the exits.

What happened in the Laigh Kirk was, by far, the more serious of the two occurrences. Fears and rumours that the structure was unsafe, and that replacement, alteration and repair had turned it into a death-trap, must have caused frequent disquiet when services were being held.

On the day disaster struck, Sunday 18th October 1801, the Laigh had a much bigger congregation than usual. The High Church was without a minister, and, being under the spiritual direction of the Laigh, the congregation flocked down to the Cross to join in the local service.

The church was nearly full as Dr. Mackinlay was making his way to the pulpit. Suddenly, a piece of plaster fell from the ceiling, a piece so small, it was later seen to be, that, even if it had hit someone, no injury would have been caused.

However, their minds at once gripped by the rumours about safety, the congregation immediately raised the cry that the building was falling apart. Panic spread like wildfire. An uncontrolled rush for the exits caused jamming of the corridors. People fainted or collapsed injured, making the situation worse by the minute. Those in the galleries made for the stairs, only to find their way down blocked by late-comers on the way up.

Bodies piled up in the mad scramble for safety. Appeals for calm by a few worshippers, who had realised that the church was in no danger, were long ignored. At last, Dr. Mackinlay managed to control the panic. The shouting, the shoving, the pushing subsided. Those who could extracted themselves from the piles of bodies on the stairs and in the corridors. The press on the doorways eased. But, when sanity returned, it served only to alert survivors to the horror of the madness which had only recently gripped them.

Thirty people lost their lives in the Laigh Kirk that afternoon in 1801. The number of injured was many times more. A catastrophic day for the Laigh and for the people of Kilmarnock generally. No wonder the church was soon the subject of a new legend, that the Devil had been seen driving a coach decorated with the sable emblems of mourning through the kirkyard.

No more sermons were preached in the Laigh. Despite the fact that the structure had not collapsed, it was found that it was not as safe as it should be. It was pulled down on 20th April, 1802, and the foundation stone of another Laigh Kirk, the present one, was laid. All that remains today of the mediaeval parish church of Kilmarnock is the lower part of the tower bearing a 15th-century date.

Not long after St. Marnock's Church was opened in 1836, rumour spread around Kilmarnock that the building was unsafe. The great width and weight of the roof raised the suspicion that the walls were sinking. Later work on the roof strengthened it in the centre, and no doubt strengthened congregational suspicion about its safety.

One Sunday morning, as Rev. David Strong was baptising a child, a gale uprooted a tree and sent it crashing into a wall of the church. So violent was the wind that one of the great doors of the church was ripped open.

As had occurred in the Laigh Kirk some 35 years earlier, fears about the safety of the roof instilled panic in the congregation. A curl of smoke coming from the Session House added to the alarm. "The Church is on fire" was heard from various parts.

In the panic which followed, women screamed and fainted. Some people collapsed in terror in the pews, forcing those still able to move to scramble over them to get to safety. Confusion reigned for some minutes; loss of life seemed inevitable.

Fortunately, Mr. Strong lived up to his name. Rushing into the pulpit, he gradually persuaded the congregation that the Church was in no danger except from panic.

When order was restored, thanks to Mr. Strong, it was quickly seen that every member of the congregation had escaped with nothing worse than a severe fright.

SANDY BY GASLIGHT

Not long after William Murdoch from Auchinleck used coal gas in 1792 to light the house where he lived in Cornwall (first time gas had been used in Britain as an illuminant), Kilmarnock became the first town in Scotland to harness gas in this way.

Hearing of Murdoch's success, Alexander (Sandy) Alexander, a cabinetmaker to trade, lit his home and workshop in the Strand with gas conducted inside by means of wooden piping.

Consumption of gas increased rapidly in Kilmarnock as houses changed to the new form of lighting. The Council's purchase of the town's private gas company back in 1871 turned out now to be a highly profitable investment.

HORSE POWER AND STEAM POWER

The tramroad, which the Duke of Portland laid down between Kilmarnock and Troon in 1808, established a number of 'firsts' for Kilmarnock and Scotland.

There had been tramroads before—at pitheads, for example. But the Duke's road was, in its day, a great feat of transport engineering. The tramroad stretched 10 miles from a loading centre near Kilmarnock House, across Shewalton Moss, to the harbour at Troon. On the way, it was carried over the River Irvine by a 4-arch bridge, the first bridge ever to carry a railway across a river.

The Duke's tramroad was constructed principally to take coal from his pits in Caprington to Troon for export. Very soon, wagons were carrying timber, grain, slates, and lime, all by simple horse-power. Passenger carriages were also introduced, making the tramroad the first passenger railway in Scotland.

With an eye to expanding business, the Duke invited George Stephenson, inventor of the steam locomotive, to try one of his 'Iron Horses' on the Kilmarnock-Troon line. Stephenson's brother, Robert, assembled a locomotive at

Kilmarnock, set it on the track, built up a working head of steam, and drove off. Though the locomotive got the length of Gargieston, the track did not suit its wheels. This, and an estimated uneconomical operating cost, made the experiment a failure. Horse-power remained unchallenged for the next 20 years. During this period, the tram road carried 200,000 tons of coal and merchandise annually to Troon and gave an immense boost to Kilmarnock industry.

In 1837, Parliament authorised conversion of the track for steam traction. Ten years later, in 1847, the Glasgow and South Western Railway obtained a lease of the Kilmarnock-Troon railway for 999 years.

HERO OF WATERLOO

The Battle of Waterloo was at its height when a Kilmarnock soldier, Sergeant Charles Ewart of the Scots Greys, performed a feat of arms which has assured him ever since of a place of high honour among the military heroes of Scotland.

Expert swordsman, Master of Fence in the Greys, Sergeant Ewart took part in a cavalry charge on Napoleon's 'Invincibles.' Accounts describe the savagery of combat with lance and sword. Kilmarnock Standard of 25th November, 1879, tells how Sergeant Ewart, in the act of cutting down a French officer, was persauded by a young Ensign to show mercy. "Take the Frenchman to the rear," he told the Ensign.

Ewart was riding off when a pistol shot caused him to look round. The Ensign was falling from his saddle, an obvious victim of his prisoner, caught in the act of putting his pistol away. Without more ado, Ewart despatched the Frenchman, as he had originally intended.

Ewart next found himself in hand-to-hand combat with a French standard-bearer. As the Frenchman fell, the Standard slipped from his grasp, rooting itself in the soft ground, thus enabling Ewart to grab it as he rode past. A spear was hurled at him by a lancer; Ewart retaliated and a third Frenchman fell to his sword.

In a letter, quoted by Archibald McKay, the Kilmarnock historian, Ewart says that he was ordered by a superior to 'take the Standard to the rear.'

"I retired to a height which gave a general view of the field," he wrote. "I cannot express the horror I felt–the bodies of my brave comrades, horses innumerable, so thick upon the field it was scarcely possible to pass".

Sergeant Ewart's prowess preceded him into Brussels, and, when he arrived there after the battle, the Belgian army greeted him with acclamation. As a reward for his valour, he was promoted Ensign in the 5th Royal Veterans.

The war over, Ensign Ewart retired to the neighbourhood of Manchester. Why to Manchester and not to Kilmarnock is not known. However, until his death in 1846 at the age of 78, he made regular visits to Kilmarnock. On these visits, he was made a Freeman of Irvine, eulogized by Sir Walter Scott in Edinburgh, and honoured at a private meeting in Kilmarnock.

Following the practice of the other towns and cities, Kilmarnock responded patriotically in celebration of the end of the Napoleonic Wars. Waterloo Street commemorates the final victory. Wellington Street was so named in honour of the Duke of Wellington, Commander of the British Army.

The frequent attempts which have been made to persuade Kilmarnock to establish some kind of memorial to Sergeant Ewart have all failed. But, there is a memorial to him on the Esplanade at Edinburgh Castle, and underneath lie his remains, re-interred there in 1938 after exhumation from his grave in Salford.

THE KILMARNOCK MARTYRS

Allowed only one vote for its 13,000 inhabitants, Kilmarnock readily joined in the popular campaign for Parliamentary reform which overlapped the end of the 18th century and the first half of the 19th.

On Saturday, 7th December, 1816, about 6,000 people attended a meeting in Dean Park called to consider petitioning the Prince Regent and the two Houses of Parliament on 'the distressed state of the country' and on the need for extension of the franchise, especially the need for better representation of the working classes.

Alexander McLaren, a local weaver, and member of a committee which organised the meeting, spoke of the "sufferings of the country" and the "narrow-minded policy of the Government." Archibald Craig drew attention to the ruinous consequences of war and the increasing burden of taxation caused by the National Debt. John Burt, who was in Paisley at the time, sent a speech describing the distress which was being suffered by working people. The army practice of punishment by flogging was highlighted by John Kennedy.

Another speaker drew attention to the fact that, of Ayrshire's 127,000 inhabitants, only 156 had the right to vote.

As a result of the Dean Park meeting, a resolution was passed pronouncing representation of Scotland in Parliament as 'unreasonable, unconstitutional and unjust.' Petitions expressing the need for Parliamentary reform, and help for those in distress, were sent to the Prince Regent, the House of Commons and the House of Lords.

It is likely that nothing more would have been heard of the meeting and the petitions had not the organising committee decided to publish the speeches and sell them to help meet the expenses of the meeting and the petitions.

Alexander McLaren and Thomas Baird, a local shopkeeper, were arrested. McLaren was charged that he did "at a public meeting in Dean Park, which meeting was attended by a great multitude of persons, chiefly of the lower orders, wickedly and feloniously deliver a speech containing seditious and inflammatory remarks and assertions, calculated to degrade and bring into contempt, the Government and legislature... and to fill the realm with trouble and dissension."

Baird was charged that, "having been present at the Dean Park meeting," and, "having heard the said speech (McLaren's) and others of similar tendency, he did wickedly and feloniously print, or cause, or procure, to be printed, at the printing office of Hugh Crawford, a seditious tract or statement."

Together, Baird and McLaren were accused of "wickedly and feloniously printing, selling, publishing and circulating the said seditious tract or statement."

Both men were found guilty. The Lord Justice-Clerk, Rt. Hon. David Boyle, sentenced both McLaren and Baird to six months imprisonment in the Tolbooth, Edinburgh, "until they shall find sufficient caution for their good behaviour for the space of three years after expiration of imprisonment." Caution of £200 sterling was required of Baird and caution of £40 required of McLaren.

Baird and McLaren did not live long after release from prison. Craig and Kennedy were imprisoned but released without charge. Craig was detained in jail for a second time but again released without charge. Both Craig and Kennedy emigrated to the U.S. Burt had to flee the country.

In 1885, a handsome Corinthian column, surmounted by a female figure symbolising liberty, was unveiled by Lord Rosebery in Kay Park. It bears the inscription: "To the memory of Thomas Baird and Alexander McLaren, as also John Burt, John Kennedy, Archibald Craig and other Kilmarnock pioneers of Parliamentary reform who, in the early part of the 19th Century, devoted themselves with unselfish zeal to the cause of the people."

From Australia and the columns of the *Melbourne Age*, dated 12th December, 1885, comes this tribute;

> It is only right that posterity should treasure the names of Alexander McLaren and Thomas Baird. These men do not belong to Scotland alone. Wherever the British race is planted in the enjoyment of constitutional liberties, their memory ought to be cherished.

THE SOUR-MILK REBELLION

In 1829 the Cross was the town's principal market place, Stalls offered anything from Black Man (a kind of licorice toffee regarded as a delicacy) to necessities such as boots, shoes, woollen apparel, pots, pans, vegetables, meat, fruit and fish.

Market Day was also the day when farmers drove their milk into town in carts for vending at the Cross. One day in 1829, without warning to the public, the farmers decided to do themselves a bit of financial good by reducing the sour-milk measure without reducing the price to consumers.

The farmers very soon paid for their trickery and for their obvious indifference to the suffering and poverty which was all around them.

Kilmarnock's women were in no mood for paying up meekly. "Back to the old measure and back to the old price," they demanded. The women threatened to "break both the jug and the head of anyone who paid the increased price."

That the threat was not an idle one was made violently clear when some women indicated they were willing to pay up. Uproar ensued as the protesters surged angrily round the farmers and their sour-milk carts. From outside the Cross, militant reinforcements were soon arriving.

The situation was inflamed when a Bailie, accompanied by the Town Officer, tried to restore order. Opening the taps of the luggies, the women filled their cans with sour milk and gleefully emptied them over the Bailie and his companion. Wherever the pair went, they were drowned in sour milk. They were soaked, and smelling something awful, when, at last, sense prevailed over misguided duty and they fled into the Town Hall. Noting that their allies were in disarray, the farmers gave in. The old measure and the old price were restored. The 'Sour Milk Rebellion' was over; the people had triumphed.

No more than a year after the 'Sour-Milk Rebellion,' the inhabitants of Kilmarnock successfully flouted another attempt to get money unfairly out of them.

For weeks, the townspeople had been looking forward to seeing Mr. Green, a popular aeronaut, ascend by balloon from the Cross. Thousands arrived for the event, only to find that the Council had barricaded all the entrances to the Cross with the intention of charging for admission.

The plan received short shrift. The barricades were pulled down, the crowd rushed into the Cross to share the best vantage points with invited guests as Mr. Green went up, up, up in his beautiful balloon.

Thirteen years after 250 Kilmarnock people died of cholera in 1832, compilers of The *Second Statistical Account of Scotland* were giving the town almost a clean bill of health.

Referring to the cholera epidemic, the *Statistical Account* (1845) notes that the proportion of deaths to population was "nearly the same as in towns of equal magnitude in other parts of Britain. The health of the parish is as good as can be looked for amidst a population of so mixed a character."

If the compilers of the *Second Statistical Account* had examined the water supply in the poorest areas of Kilmarnock where most of the cholera deaths occurred, they might not have been so smug about public health. Principal source of water round about the Cross was the Town Well. Straight into the well water went the fluid from two tanning pits close by.

Pollution of the Town Well by the tanning yards must have been a major cause of the 1832 cholera epidemic. In 1849, just four years after the *Second Statistical Account* had published its inaccurate account of the health of the town, another 130 people had died from cholera in Kilmarnock.

The disease made its last appearance in Kilmarnock in 1854. By then, much of the town was enjoying a supply of gravitation water laid on from Rowallan Estate by a private company. Only 34 deaths occurred in the final cholera epidemic.

Cholera monument in Howard Park.

Kilmarnock Town Council took over the Rowallan water supply in 1892. Between then and 1910, new catchment areas at Fenwick, Craigendunton and Loch Goin had given the whole of Kilmarnock a wholesome supply of water. Construction of a screening plant at Meadowhead in 1934 helped to clean up the River Irvine by piping treated sewage to the coast.

Whether or not Kilmarnock owes its origin all these centuries back to a Saintly Christian Monk from Ireland remains to this day a fascinating mystery. But, there is no doubt that the first settlers in the area which is now the town of Kilmarnock stopped here because of the abundance of water.

Where better to settle than at, or near to, the confluence of two rivers?

The Kilmarnock Water, plenished below its head waters by many vigorous streams, flows through Kilmarnock to join the greater River Irvine at Gargieston.

Water, water, everywhere, therefore, but, at a price, Kilmarnock has learned.

Two disastrous floods have hit the town in the past 137 years. In just two hours early on the morning of 14th July, 1852, a violent rainstorm caused the tributaries of the Kilmarnock Water to overflow. A torrent seven feet deep roared into Townholm, destroying bridges and uprooting huge boulders.

Townholm Foundry was destroyed: the inhabitants had to flee their homes and take refuge on high ground, as the flood powered its way towards Kilmarnock Cross.

The narrow Flesh Market Bridge acted more like a dam than a water channel. Water level rose so sharply that, within minutes, the Cross was under deep and deepening water.

Archibald McKay, the local historian, tells of men, women and children running in all directions, searching for safety above the water, of tenants knocking down the walls of their houses to get out, of prisoners rescued from their cells in the Tolbooth.

Diverging at the Cross, the torrent swept along Sandbed and down King Street and Titchfield Street before becoming one stream again at Douglas Street. Water level reached almost six feet. Houses, shops, bridges, suffered enormous damage. Over 200 families, 90 of them the poorest in the town, were left destitute.

Bearing in mind the cataclysmic effect which the 1852 flood had on the poorest citizens of Kilmarnock, it is ironic to note a claim that the havoc was the result of successful land care.

Mr. McKay quotes a Sir Thomas Dick Lander: "Any given quantity of rain must now produce a much greater flood than it could have done before the country became so improved."

"When we consider the number of open cuts made to dry out hill pasture, the numerous bogs reclaimed by drainage, the ditches of enclosure, the roads formed with side drains and cross conduits, we shall find... that the country has been covered with a perfect network of courses to catch and concentrate raindrops as they fall and hurry them off, in the accumulated tribute, to the next stream."

A sound enough conclusion, no doubt, and, with drain tiles by the million being manufactured in Ayrshire, some effective measures to prevent serious flooding in future ought to have been put into effect by the authorities. They certainly did take action of a kind, but only to request the townspeople not to block the Kilmarnock Water by dumping rubbish into it.

The flood had a grim sequel. Townholm legend told of a pit accident between 1840 and 1850 which had claimed the lives of eight colliers. The rush of water through Townholm during the 1852 flood uncovered the shaft of a pit. Eleven years later, in 1863, examination of the pit floor revealed several skeletons with antique implements of labour close by.

Kilmarnock continued to be beset by flooding, much of it in the over-crowded south-western districts. Floods are recorded in 1888, 1904, 1911, 1932, 1953 and 1958.

The 1932 flood, by far the worst, fortunately did not have such serious effect upon our most vulnerable citizens as had the one in 1852.

As the result of heavy rain from Hogmanay in 1931 to the 3rd January 1932, serious flooding occurred in the lower areas of Kilmarnock when both the Kilmarnock and the Irvine overflowed. More than 150 families had to be rescued in horse-drawn carts. Men used boats to rescue sheep from flooded fields off Queens Drive. Firemen pumped water 18 feet deep from the Power Station. The Glenfield, Barr Thomsons and other factories were also flooded.

To make matters worse, the Cessnock burst its banks, surging through Riccarton Moss, and carrying thousands of tons of sludge along the railway from Hurlford to Riccarton. Pumping was stopped at the Power Station. The electric lights of Kilmarnock went out, to be replaced by candles until power was restored a day later.

Thanks to the efforts of the Town Council and voluntary organisations, all the victims were accommodated in halls. Gifts of coal and charcoal from the Council helped to dry out the flooded houses. Workers in factories and other premises, which suffered flood damage, were given an extended New Year holiday so that cleaning-up could be completed.

The great social distress caused by the 1932 flood was once again met with demands for action to protect the low-lying parts of the town. This time, some effective measures were taken. Work was stepped up on raising the height of the embankments of the River Irvine between Struthers Steps and the Victoria Bridge at the town entrance to Queens Drive. Industrial waste from the Glenfield and waste from other sources gradually tamed the river. In Riccarton, dredging was begun to remove silt from the bed of the Irvine and widen the channels under the bridges.

The 1932 flood set a Kilmarnock couple thinking about the flood which destroyed the world in 40 days and 40 nights. During the week of the flood, a son was born to Mr. and Mrs. Samuel Thompson, 31 Low Glencairn Street. The child was at once baptised Noah Dunsmuir Thompson at a Salvation Army service in the Thompsons house.

TOWER, OBSERVATORY AND CASTLE

Thomas Morton, a native of Mauchline, was only three years of age when he was brought by his father to Kilmarnock in 1786. There he was to live and work for most of the rest of his life.

With an eye to his future security, Morton learned the trades of bricklaying (his father's trade) and turner-wheelwright during the day. Night classes gave him a sound educational back-up.

But, it wasn't as a tradesman that Morton was to excel. He had a natural genius for mechanics and was particularly interested in the study and manufacture of scientific instruments.

The 'geography' and mathmetics of the universe fascinated him and turned his attention towards the telescope. Whenever he could, he examined the instrument in detail. In those days, the early 1800s, Italians regularly visited Britain to sell telescopes and barometers. Having no money, Morton used his persuasive tongue to induce the salesmen to let him examine their telescopes. Nothing escaped him about their construction: the faults which he noted immediately suggested to his mind the improvements they needed.

The first telescope Thomas Morton made was good enough to be put into service in an astronomical observatory which he built for himself at the top of the Gas Brae for £1,000. Two more telescopes followed, one a 9⅜″ Newtonian, the other a 7″ Gregorian, both excellent instruments of their kind, and recognised as such by astronomers of the day.

Visitors to Morton's observatory were many. Besides being able to see the sky at night, they could enjoy the pleasure of viewing the surrounding countryside through a camera obscura, constructed by Morton.

Established in business now, Morton began to work on improving carpet manufacture. From his workshop came the revolutionary barrel carpet machine, the 3-ply carpet machine, the Brussels carpet machine which worked five colours from four needles, and improvements to the Jacquard loom. Thanks to the Morton carpet machines and improvements, 1200 weavers found stable employment in the manufacture of carpets, 'the quality and pattern of which are not surpassed by any others in Britain.'

In recognition of the great contribution Morton had made to Britain's manufacturing power, the Board of Trade awarded him a grant. A similar gesture was made to him by the manufacturers of Kilmarnock.

After Morton's death in 1862, the Observatory was continued in use by Mr James Kilmurray, or, as he was better known, 'Auld Killie, the weather prophet.' Here, in what was now called Killie's Castle, Mr Kilmurray searched the sky with the Morton telescopes, gathering information which he applied to weather forecasting. Whether or not Auld Killie's predictions owed anything to his telescopic sky trek no one will ever know. But they were popular enough to be published regularly in local and Glasgow newspapers, and to find favour with farmers.

Morton Tower.

Auld Killie worked long and hard for the troops during the Great War of 1914-18. No man could have done more to see that they were supplied with all material comforts. Out to the battlefields went a constant flow of goods:- pipes, cigarettes, tobacco, clothing, food, soap, brushes, razors, hair clippers, even banjoes, melodeons, concertinas, mouth organs, walking sticks, crutches and artificial legs.

The war over, Kilmarnock and its soldiers expressed thanks to Auld Killie by sending him on a tour of the battlefields of France. Before he died in December 1926, failing health had forced him to leave his 'castle' to live in Titchfield Street.

Morton Observatory, alias Killie's Castle, was pulled down in 1958 to make way for new housing.

EXCELSIOR, THE STORY OF THE CO-OP

Motivated by the belief that co-operation is, and always will be, superior to competition, a small band of Kilmarnock men came together in May, 1860, to establish the town's first co-operative society.

Right from the start, the Co-op became the staff of life for thousands of people. It raised them above the poverty line which they had occupied all their lives, and their fathers, mothers and grandparents before them, and provided them with goods and services at prices well below what they had to pay to private traders. The more they bought from the Co-op, the more they got in dividend. From profits came reading rooms to inform and educate, capital for house loans, education to university standard, for holidays and for helping members out of financial trouble.

When the Society celebrated its 50th anniversary in 1910, it had destroyed the myth that working people were incapable of making successful businessmen.

In a preface to William Robertson's *Fifty years of Co-operation in Kilmarnock,* James Deans proudly points to the marked success of the Society.

"Success forms conclusive proof," said Mr. Deans, "that the wage-earning classes are not an inferior species of the race but are the equal of any other section of society in their ability to organise, to legislate, and to administer. It would not be easy to name another movement or institution which has done more to make it possible for a working man to brave the blows of circumstance and grapple with his evil star."

Kilmarnock, in 1860, was continuing the struggle for extension of the franchise and better conditions for working people, a struggle which had been strengthened more than weakened by the imprisonment of Baird and McLaren in 1817 for selling a seditious pamphlet. In various parts of the town, as in many parts of Scotland, particularly the Lowlands, men and women came together regularly to hear the news of the day and discuss mutual problems. Those, who could read, read newspapers and pamphlets to those who couldn't. Cost was shared in proportion to means.

One Sunday in August, 1860, members of one of these groups sat themselves down in the pleasant company of Craufurdland Bridge to talk, as they had done so often in the past, about the things that matter. With the wellbeing of the masses to inspire them, they readily agreed to a suggestion that a co-operative society, like the one which had recently been formed in Rochdale, should be formed in Kilmarnock. Profits would be divided in relation to purchases, not on capital holdings.

The following month, September, Kilmarnock Equitable Co-operative Society came into being in a rented room in Princes Street. Membership at the start was 13, capital £1 3s 6d. Two nights a week, the Princes Street premises were opened for members to buy tea, sugar and tobacco – much cheaper than they would get them elsewhere.

Progress was so great that, only a year after its beginning, the Society had to take over bigger premises in Cheapside Street. By the end of the last quarter of the year, sales had risen from £50 to £231, membership from 20 to 80, and a profit of £24 16s 10d had been made.

More progress in 1863 encouraged the Society to move into more spacious premises in Waterloo Street. The Board, in what could almost be described as an Order of the Day, extolled with unwavering conviction the high ideals of co-operation.

"Co-operation", they said, "will emancipate labour, abolish strikes, solve the problem how we, the toilers of this country, may justly profit by our own skill and industry. It aims at elevating men morally, socially, physically, and politically by freeing us from the poverty and wretchedness which chain millions to an animal existence."

In their Order of the Day, at the close of a successful third year, the Board called upon the people of Kilmarnock to join the Co-op and "rejoice together in the dawn of a brighter day for the sons of labour."

"Who would that want and woe should cease
And love and truth and joy increase,
Who would behold the reign of peace:
Co-operate! Co-operate!"

The growing popularity of the Society must have strengthened the Board's belief that Co-operation was the panacea for all social ills, that it would bring to working men wealth, advancement, comfort of mind and body, intellectual culture–in short, everything that was good and great. Not only did they preach the gospel of Co-operation to Kilmarnock people generally, but they also dropped a word in the ears of the Co-op employees to give all their time to the Society, to balance their accounts, to report receipt of inferior goods, and not to lounge about.

It shows the Board's high principles to hear them tell members to make sure that all motions passed at meetings were put into effect. Members had no difficulty keeping in touch with decisions. The rules required that all business should be minuted, and, if approved, put into effect.

Awareness that the Society was the sum-total of its members, and that members were the Society, dominated business relations. A member could quickly get his £2 capital back simply by asking. If he didn't need all his capital, he could get a loan of some smaller sum. "Small matters perhaps," said Mr. Robertson, "but illustrative of the vicissitudes and tragedies that frequently make life so hard for the great bulk of people."

By the end of 1870, the 10th year of its existence, the Society had opened two new branches, added to the library, and formed a loan society; capital and profits were soaring, groceries, footwear and drapery were thriving.

The decade 1871-1880 saw continuing improvement and more new branches. In 1879, the Society proudly revealed its prosperity with the opening of modern central premises in John Finnie Street and John Dickie Street at a cost of £4,164. An extension ten years later (1889) took the total cost of the new Co-op H.Q. to £18,000.

When the Society came of age in 1881, Kilmarnock people had put their trust in it. Membership increased rapidly and, while dividends continued to be used to eke out very small family incomes, capital increased enough to permit a regular improvement in service. By the end of 1890, thirteen branches were doing business in Kilmarnock–groceries, bakers, footwear, fleshing, drapery and millinery. Sales had risen to almost £63,000 for the year and membership to 2,185.

Up and up went membership, sales and profits. A jewellery and furniture store was opened, Riccarton Institute was bought and converted into the Co-op's second reading-room for members, a building department was opened with capital of £10,000 for lending to members wanting a house of their own. An Education Committee arranged socials, stage shows, trips, cookery demonstrations, and flower shows. Women looked after their own special interests in their own guild.

By the time the Society was celebrating its jubilee in 1910, not even world trade depression could prevent it from continuing to prosper. From its start in 1860 with a membership of 13 and capital of £1 3s 6d, Kilmarnock Equitable Co-operative Society had firmly established itself more than a match for its private rivals. Membership had risen to 7,890, sales to over £212,000 and profit to £21,000. The faith of the pioneers in the business ability of ordinary working people had been pointedly demonstrated.

Today, the Kilmarnock Society is part of Ayrshire Regional Co-operative Society.

SOUP KITCHENS AND LODGING HOUSES

To the lasting credit of James Arbuckle, appointed a Bailie of Kilmarnock in 1878, he was to be known more for his work among the poor, his kindness to them, than for the judgements he pronounced from the Bench upon any who had gone 'a kennin wrang.'

Bailie Arbuckle believed that it was his duty to see that those who were unable to provide for themselves were not allowed to go hungry.

In the Corporation Soup Kitchen in Nelson Street, Bailie Arbuckle handed out to the hungry and the destitute of Kilmarnock the manna which he collected from the town's butchers, bakers, grocers and other suppliers of food. He never met with a refusal, indication that the town's better-off citizens shared his concern for the poor.

Preparation of the food, and its division into meals of equal size, was shared by the Bailie, an old soldier friend named Hugh Paton, and two women. Principal course, as you would expect, was soup, very often thick Scotch broth which 'stuck to your ribs.'

About mid-day, the door of the Soup Kitchen was opened and in crowded men, women, children, the very young and the very old. Billycans and corn-beef cans were presented, and into them went the broth, and sometimes, to save space and labour, the ration of beef as well. The meal was completed with two slices of bread. Those who arrived without receptacles were supplied with bowls and were often allowed to enjoy their meal in the warmth of the kitchen.

Besides his three helpers, Bailie Arbuckle could rely, without fail, upon a woman across the road to provide shelter, table, and cutlery for any diners who could not be accommodated in the kitchen.

The Soup Kitchen was the keystone of the Council's relief services. It was under the jurisdiction of a Council sub-committee; the practice was to bring it into use in times of extreme hardship, say, from unemployment, or strike, fire or weather.

The Nelson Street Soup Kitchen was closed in 1883, but another was opened in its place in Waterside Street. This one was certainly in use right up to the start of the 1939-45 war. Since the end of the war, poverty, destitution, strikes and natural catastrophes have periodically required the authorities, and working-class organisations, to open the soup kitchens again. The Bailie Arbuckles are still needed 100 years after he fed the poor in Nelson Street.

Supplementing the soup kitchens in the town's poor-relief services there were the lodging houses. About the turn of the century, some twelve or thirteen of these common lodginghouses, as they were officially called, provided beds for over 700 sleepers a year, many of them itinerant Irishmen working as navvies, drainers, tattie howkers, harvesters, and the like. Accommodation provided no more than a place to lie on, and some sheets and blankets. The story was not uncommon that, when beds were all taken up, latecomers could sleep on their feet, draped over a rope strung between two opposite walls.

Two 'model' lodginghouses built in 1878, one in Soulis Street, the other in Ladeside Street, improved upon the accommodation offered by their common rivals. The Soulis Street Model ended its useful life as a further-education college. This one and the one in Ladeside Street were demolished in the early 1970s.

A PIONEERING BICYCLIST

This year, the 150th anniversary of the invention of the bicycle, we look back 110 years to an epic trip which was made from Kilmarnock to London and back.

A week or two before the Fair Holiday of 1878, a group of Kilmarnock friends had decided to use the break by taking the train south to Sheffield on business.

"I'll go by bicycle," said 17-year-old John Rankin. No need to labour the fact that John had been a keen cyclist for years. Often of late, he had talked with others about cycling to London and back. The business trip south was now his chance.

No one, not even his mother, could persuade John to give up the idea. The cycle trip was given approval. John's friends would leave Kilmarnock a day later by train, and meet up with him en route, if possible.

John Rankin carefully prepared his Coventry-built Haynes and Jeffrey Tangent for the trip. On to the saddle and backbone, he strapped a portmanteau containing oil can, shirt and collar, stockings, handkerchiefs, collapsible drinking cup, notebook and pencil. And off he went from the Corn Exchange at 4.15 a.m. on 23rd July 1878.

Travelling by way of Carlisle, Kendal and Skipton (the rail route) he rejoined his friends at Sheffield. Reason for the business trip is given in a report which says, the friends "visited the largest spoon and fork factory in Sheffield and met people they had done business with for 20 years." They were clearly in the cutlery retail trade. A stop-over at Coventry allowed John to see over the Haynes & Jeffrey factory where his bicycle had been made.

Resuming his journey, John passed through Birmingham and Coventry and arrived in London at 5 p.m. on 1st August—439 miles in under ten days.

John took the eastern road home—Grantham, Wetherby, Morpeth, Edinburgh, Glasgow, Kilmarnock—448 miles this time in one day less than for the trip south.

A remarkable journey of 887 miles on a bicycle of the highest pedigree. "Not a spoke, not a nut, needed tightening," said John.

THE GREAT HOAX

There was nothing in the letter which Kilmarnock Town Council received from Mr. Hew Morrison of the Public Free Library in Edinburgh to give them the slightest cause for suspicion.

Only the year before, 1903, Andrew Carnegie, the Dunfermline-born U.S. steel magnate and philanthropist, had been honoured with the Freedom of the Burgh when he laid the foundation stone of the new Loanhead Primary

School. His expressed liking and respect for the town and its citizens had council breasts swelling with pride.

So, when Provost James Hood announced at the Council meeting on Wednesday, 10th February, 1904, that Mr. Carnegie wanted to spend £500,000 on building a Burns Temple in the town, the Council accepted the gift with pleasure. The free site Mr. Carnegie asked for was promised; the conditions he laid down were found acceptable.

In his letter to the Council, Mr. Morrison, agent for Mr. Carnegie in Scotland, wrote:

> I have just received word that Mr. Carnegie was so deeply impressed with the progressive tendencies of Kilmarnock during his recent visit that he has had under consideration a project of more closely identifying the town with the name of our national Bard.
>
> Mr. Carnegie recognises Kilmarnock as the nucleus of Burns lore where the peerless poems were first published… and where all literature associated with his honoured name has been carefully compiled and disseminated.
>
> Mr. Carnegie has decided, therefore, to erect, at his own expense, within the town of Kilmarnock, a temple to the memory of our national pride, provided the Council grant a free site.   It is Mr. Carnegie's intention to make this memorial a most elaborate one, the building to be constructed of granite, white marble, or some other superior material, and to be of magnificent design, while the interior will contain statues of Burns's contemporaries and the principal characters of his creation, and, under the dome, a chaste figure of the immortal genius will stand.
>
> Artistic panels will embellish the walls, illustrative of scenes depicted in the poems, and the whole building will be lavishly created at a cost not exceeding £500,000.
>
> While Mr. Carnegie will retain, in his own hands, the plans and details of construction, he wishes the management of the Temple to be vested in a Committee of Trustees, consisting of the Provost, Magistrates and three of the people's representatives in the Council; the president and vice-president, secretary and three members of the Burns Federation; the president, vice-president and three members of Kilmarnock Burns Club; and the editor of the Burns Chronicle.
>
> In selecting a site, Mr. Carnegie has confidence in the judgement of the Kilmarnock Town Council, but, when in Kilmarnock, he was impressed with a commanding position at the entrance of your park (Kay Park) opposite to Tam Samson's House, where the imposing flights of steps could be led up to the structure, and thus add to the effect.
>
> Mr. Carnegie will be glad to learn if the Town Council are prepared to entertain the conditions of the gift, so that he can make the necessary arrangements immediately for proceeding therewith.

The Carnegie letter having been accepted as genuine, local press correspondents lost no time noising it abroad. Every national daily received the news, all the principal Scottish evening papers as well, and the news agencies with their international links.

Early in the morning of Thursday, 11th February, the day after the Council meeting, word was fed back to the local correspondents, first of all from the Scotsman, then quickly from other Scottish newspapers, that the Carnegie letter was a hoax. When asked by the Scottish newspapers for comment on Mr. Carnegie's generous gift to Kilmarnock, Mr. Morrison was less than amused. He had written no such letter to the Town Council, he said. In a letter later in the day to the Council, Mr. Morrison offered his sympathy. "It was a wretched and silly hoax," he said. "An insult to the town of Kilmarnock. The writer must have had knowledge of Mr. Carnegie's appreciation of Kilmarnock, but the rest of the letter was not characteristic of Mr. Carnegie. Especially silly was the part regarding the structure of the temple and its composition."

Bailie Munro's repentance.

25

Thursday, 11th February, 1904, was an unforgettable 'day after the night before' for Kilmarnock. The local press correspondents worked through the night advising the newspapers and news agencies of the hoax. But the magnitude of the story had already encouraged most of the media to let it out. Many newspapers appeared with the bald announcement of the Carnegie benefaction, some appeared with the announcement and a paragraph of denial tacked on at the end. Many more printed the story on its true merits–as a hoax, the great hoax, as it was to become known.

The Hoax was to be top-of-the-column, often lead copy, in the press for a year. It was not until the Council hit the headlines again by starting up its own electric tram system that the hoax began to lose interest as news and as a conversation piece.

Mr. Morrison's revelation caused acute embarrassment to the Council. No-one saw anything funny in the hoax, and the general feeling throughout the town was sympathetic towards the Council. The hoaxer had exercised his sense of fun mischievously, and, in doing so, had brought shame upon the town, its Council and upon Scotland's National Bard.

The calling of a special meeting of the Council, to institute plans aimed at identifying the hoaxer, was not long delayed. Some sections of the press used this development to chide Kilmarnock as a community lacking in humour. This was the opinion of a London paper, and the Boston News in the United States. Those who found Kilmarnock's embarrassment amusing and beguiling expressed themselves in a spate of very poor verse, jokes, cartoons, and innuendo.

Bloody but unbowed, the Council went on the attack. With the help of an official who had something of the Sherlock Holmes about him, the typewriter used for the hoax letter was traced to the police office. Sergeant Martin admitted typing the letter at the request of a magistrate, and that was how he justified his action later to the Chief Constable.

Provost Hood soon announced to the Council and lieges that the hoaxer had been identified and had given him £50 as a donation to Kilmarnock Infirmary in reparation for his misdoing. The Provost hoped this would see an end of the affair.

The Provost's hopes were confined to himself. Even allowing for the possibility that the hoaxer had meant no harm, the general view was that his identity had to be uncovered, if only to clear the name of some who were being wrongly accused.

In response to public demand, as it were, Bailie William Munro, partner in a local jam-making firm, admitted that he was the hoaxer. He had intended no malice, nor had he desired or expected that things would go as far as they had.

The Bailie apologised "with sincere regret" for his actions. He had already made handsome reparation of £50, he reminded the Council.

Reparation or no, Bailie Munro tendered his resignation from the Council. In April, two months after sending the Carnegie hoax letter to the Council, Bailie Munro was succeeded as member for Kilmarnock's Fifth Ward by Mr. John Carnie.

Practical joking was far from Bailie Munro's only talent. In more responsible mood, he enjoyed writing poetry and prose. As it was to turn out, he was also a determined survivor.

For the next month or two, ex-Bailie Munro, as he was now, kept clear of the limelight. By June, however, Kilmarnock Standard had noted his presence, significantly so, at a lecture on 'The lost tribes of Israel.' Kilmarnock Herald noted his work as secretary to Howard Park Old Men's Cabin and his contribution to arranging the annual trip to Troon.

The Bailie was back in business. In October, he offered himself as a candidate for the Fifth Ward in the elections due on 1st November. Personal arrogance and conceit, and an unworthy contempt for the Town Council, gave a caustic flavour to a re-election speech in Riccarton Institute. "I am here at your request," he said, "to thank you for letting me have my say in certain matters that have affected Kilmarnock, or, rather,have wounded those who profess to uphold the dignity of our town, but who have yet to learn how to conduct themselves in dignity."

"I have never ceased to consider myself your representative... I don't claim to be above the average in wisdom, and would never think of advocating that the Council should be composed of twenty-five Bailie Munros. But I am sure you will agree with me that, if it were so constituted, more business would be transacted and there would be less nonsense than there has been these last number of years."

Ex-Bailie Munro topped the poll in the Fifth Ward and returned to Council duties less than eight months after bringing about his own resignation by his misguided sense of humour.

Kilmarnock Herald pronounced fitting judgement on him: "No-one can be blamed for the affair except the author. It is likely the perpetrator of the hoax never anticipated that his joke would go so far. It is all very well for a joker to get his wit out, but it is infamous that a town should be made the laughing-stock of the world because of one fool's craving for fun."

HENRY SHIELDS
MASTER OF DOGGEREL

Henry Shields was an artist of great accomplishment in the composition of doggerel.

Born in Ireland, Henry lived in a house at the corner of High Street and Dean Lane in Kilmarnock. Some said he had lived in Ardrossan before coming to Kilmarnock, hence the popular habit of referring to him as Henry Shields of Kildrossan.

Though little above five feet in height, looking like an authentic leprechaun, Henry could be big when he needed.

Part of Henry's house was converted into a shop which he stuffed with a quaint assortment of Black Man, honey, matches (Lucifers), heel tackits, strippet balls, and the kind of peppermints sometimes called church liqueurs.

Henry Shield's House and Shop.

One night, the Old High minister called upon Henry to ask him to give up his practice of opening his shop on Sunday morning.

"It would let you get to Church, yourself, Henry," said the minister, craftily.

"Maybe it would," said Henry. "But I'll just keep the shop open as usual on Sunday. I wouldn't like to let the folk go without their sweeties. They tell me it's easier to thole a drab sermon if they have a sweetie to suck."

Those who decry the talent of Henry Shields and similar odd composers make the mistake, perhaps, of comparing him with the creators of orthodox verse or prose. How much do we remember, or want to remember, of the sonnets of Shakespeare, what was Cicero pontificating about in the market place, what, in all conscience, did Juliet mean when she asked Romeo wherefor he was.

Henry Shields is immediately understandable, which makes him superior as a communicator, say, to politicians whose cliche-ridden utterances leave their audiences drowning in a sea of verbal treacle. Every spade in the potting shed of Henry's mind is, clearly, a spade.

Often the victim of practical jokes, Henry believed to the day he died that a letter which he received from Germany had been written by Bismarck. In the letter, the Iron Chancellor complimented Henry on the quality of his poems, and expressed a particular fondness for the one about Mr. Marwood, the hangman:

Oh, here comes Mr. Marwood with his swivel and his rope.
And he whispered to Dan Curly "will you please hold up your throat."
He touched the lever with his foot,
And to the bottom he did go.

Memorable verse there is no doubt about that. But what were the names of the holiday jokers?

The military funeral of Sergeant-Major Flynn of the local volunteers in 1891 was saluted in immortal verse by Henry. (Sgt. Flynn was drowned when fishing at Mauchline.)

The water deep comes round the sweep,
    It's fu' o' mud an' glaur,
And Sergeant Flynn being venturesome
    Went into it too faur.

It was on the 27th of October
    His funeral took place:
It was the longest I have seen
    In all the human race.

The 21st—they made a burst
    For to get through the gate:
The Rifles followed after—
    They were afraid they would be late.

A few years after Kay Park Loch opened in 1879, punts, rowing boats and canoes were launched on the water. Henry showed his appreciation thus:

As I went down the Kay Park Walk,
    I could scarcely give a cough—
Four-and-twenty pleasure boats
    Were sailing on the Loch.

The similarity between Henry Shields and William McGonigale is seen in their shared interest in the Tay Railway Bridge.

When the original bridge collapsed in 1879, Henry mourned:

Twas on the 28th of December,
Right well do I remember
The night was very stormy, and the bridge it did give way,
And that's the reason why so many are buried in the Tay.

Opening of the second Tay Railway Bridge in 1882, was greeted rapturously by McGonigale:

Beautiful railway bridge of the River Tay,
That has caused the Emperor of Brazil to leave
His home far away, incognito in his breast,
And view thee ere he passed along en route for Inverness.

On 18th August, 1966, H.M. Queen Elizabeth opened the new Tay Road Bridge. Travellers had to pay tolls to cross. Under the influence of William and Henry, both gone now but not forgotten, the writer of Local echoes, in the Kilmarnock Standard kept their memories alive:

The Tay Bridge is far from Kilmarnock but—
For those who go from here to Dundee, it will be a fine short cut:
Thousands will cross it every day in shoals,
And there would be many more, I have no doubt, if it weren't for the tolls.

Hail to the Henry Shields and the William McGonigales, Poets Laureate to all the doggerel lovers of the world.

THE TRAMS HAD A GOOD RUN

Born in 1904 of a community confident in its industrial strength, Kilmarnock Corporation Tramways system was robust enough in childhood to suggest that a long life lay ahead. Alas, the child was unexpectedly stricken by industrial disease and succumbed to it not long after coming of age.

A look at events before the first tram trundled into service suggests, with hindsight, of course, that the Council may have acted with a degree of foolhardiness. Expert opinion which was far from confident about success did nothing to shake the Council. Nor did an unfavourable plebiscite. According to the Council, the ambiguous nature of the questions put to ratepayers entitled them to claim the tramway system had public support. And they underlined the faith they had in their own judgement by turning down requests from Irvine, Galston, Newmilns and Darvel to join in the tramways scheme.

The Act of Parliament giving Kilmarnock Town Council authority to go ahead with a combined lighting and traction scheme was given Royal assent in 1903. Work was started at once on construction of an electric power station on the north bank of the River Irvine at Riccarton. By October, 1903, overhead power lines had been fixed and tramlines laid. On 10th December, Lord Howard de Walden set the trams rolling by driving the first one along the two routes–Beansburn burgh boundary to Riccarton and Kilmarnock Cross to Hurlford Cross. All the track (4½ miles) was single except for the section running through the town's main shopping centre from West High Church in the north to King Street Church in the south. This section which was two-track was later extended to the tram sheds of Riccarton. Passing loops were constructed every half-mile on the single-track sections.

The 'Skoosh cars' or 'Sparkies,' as the trams were quickly dubbed, enjoyed the early success which often comes from novelty. The initial 11 cars were increased by two, Sunday services and workmen's tickets were introduced. By the end of 1907, the trams were still busy and the balance sheet was still showing profit. Ominously, repairs to the permanent way were proving more and more expensive.

By 1910, the novelty of the trams was wearing off. Success of the power station wasn't enough to offset the deficit on the trams. The 1914-18 war brought insoluble problems. Repairs to track were frequent and expensive, overhead wire had often to be spliced instead of replaced. Growing competition from motor buses and renewed public interest in horse-drawn transport made the end of the trams inevitable. In the hope of cashing in on the popularity of the motor buses, the Council put four Thorneycrofts and four Albions on the road.

The motor buses were too late to save the trams. The General Strike of 1926 confined them to their sheds at Riccarton, and, when the strike ended after ten days, the Council decided not to put them back into service. The day of the 'Sparkies' was over in Kilmarnock. Behind them they left not unpleasant memories of an ambitious project–and a deficit of £50,000 on 22 years working.

Track was soon lifted, overhead wires were dismantled and the trams sold. Two trams were sold to Ayr: others ended up as huts and stores in farms and smallholdings.

BOBBY IN THE LION'S DEN

Bobby Templeton, famous Scottish football internationalist in the late 19th and early 20th centuries, was a lad of pairts, if ever there was one.

Capped many times for Scotland, he had the reputation of being the greatest footballer of his day. Besides Kilmarnock, he played for Aston Villa, Newcastle United, and Woolwich (later Arsenal). To Scotland, he was what Stanley Mathews was to become to England in the 1950s.

Collapse of timber terracing at Ibrox during an international between Scotland and England in 1902 caused the deaths of 25 people. To this day, it is believed it was the cantraips of Templeton and Bobby Walker of Hearts on Scotland's right wing that caused the fans to lean forward, thus transferring their weight to a weak part of the terracing and causing the collapse.

As 'mine host' of the Royal Hotel in Duke Street when he played for Kilmarnock, Bobby encouraged the footballing fraternity to drop in. One night when football topics had been exhausted, Bobby showed a boastful side of himself by engaging in a £5 wager that he would go into the lion's cage in a menagerie then visiting Kilmarnock.

Not many people thought Bobby was serious, but turn up he did on the appointed day. The menagerie was full. Someone delivered an elaborate oration in Bobby's honour. Quietly he was assisted up the steps into the lion's cage. A spectator describes the scene: "It was evident the lion had been doped. It just lay in a corner bleary-eyed, looking as if it was nearing its end. Bobby looked bleary-eyed as well."

For a couple of minutes, footballer and lion eyed each other disinterestedly. Feeling some tension even though this could hardly have been a result of the confrontation in the cage, the crowd waited for the next move. At last, on a signal from Bobby, the cage was opened and out he stepped to pick up £5, and to receive the over-generous applause of the crowd.

John Thornton, our observer, was convinced that the lion never saw Bobby, nor Bobby the lion.

"YOU'LL NEVER WALK ALONE"
The author salutes the gemme

In the late 1920s when I was still at Loanhead elementary school, Kilmarnock was one vast football playground. Street gangs formed themselves into teams, playing one another in the parks and streets. The 'tanner ba" was popular with street footballers, but, those who couldn't afford one, made do with a ball of paper and string, or an empty can. Goal posts were formed of jackets, or jerseys, placed on the road about 15 feet apart.

School playgrounds became football fields before and after hours, at playtime and dinner time. Teams took part in a schools league which was popular with fans generally.

The Schools Cup Final at Rugby Park was attended every year by thousands of spectators. Many a footballer, who learned the skills of football at school, went on to play for senior clubs. Stars such as James (Bud) Maxwell, Jimmy Falconer, Alan Collins, Dougie McAvoy and Freddy Milloy went on to play for Kilmarnock.

District Leagues were formed from teams like Newton Rovers, Riccarton and Netherton. Glenfield, Barclay's, Walker's, and BMK fielded teams in an inter-works league. The Glenfield had enough workers, over 2000 in its heyday, to form department teams exclusively engaged in their own works league. A Churches League catered for teams in Kilmarnock and surrounding towns and villages.

I had just been born when Kilmarnock beat Albion Rovers 3-2 to win the Scottish Cup in 1920. Nine years later, Kilmarnock won the Cup again, this time defeating Glasgow Rangers 2-0 at Hampden before a crowd of 114,000. As soon as Jimmy Williamson clinched victory over Rangers by adding a second goal to Daddler Aitken's opener, pigeons rose from the terracings and winged their way back to Kilmarnock with the news.

Though too young to attend the match at Hampden, I was lucky enough to be taken by my mother to the Cross to join the thousands who had gathered to welcome the victors home. As the corporation fire engine, carrying the team and the Cup, moved slowly down Portland Street and through the Cross to the Town Hall, Jimmy Shaw, Kilmarnock's carrara-marble *Dick Whittington,* bowed to Captain Mattha Smith and the Scottish Cup. I know because I was there.

Rugby Park has been a Mecca for me ever since that Scottish Cup victory in 1929. Very soon, I joined the hoards of weans who, every Saturday afternoon, gathered at the town end of Rugby Park hoping to get in free. "Gie's a lift ower, sir, gie's a lift ower, sir, please." The call was heard scores of times at every big team match. Along with thousands of other Kilmarnock weans, that is how I got into Rugby Park for many a year.

Another way of getting into the 'gemme' at Rugby Park without paying was on the 'hauf-time special.' Those who didn't manage a 'lift ower' waited well into the second half. About 20 minutes from the end, the gates were opened and in rushed the hauf-time special.

Saturday afternoons were exclusively football afternoons. Minor games that day were planned with the starting time at Rugby Park in mind. In those days, when there was no floodlighting, games started at 2 p.m. On Lesser Rugby Park, ground now used as a car park, Kilmarnock Academicals started their games at 2.15. This allowed them to get two or three hundred fans from the big game to spend half-time watching them. Many fans migrated to the Accies ground again as soon as the 'big game' ended.

And that wasn't the end of football Saturday. The big game over, and the Accies game over, the fans went home by way of Howard Park. Here, they were often in time for the last few minutes of a juvenile game. Not a trick was missed. As the fans from Rugby Park were arriving, out came the bonnet and a collection was taken for the wee clubs.

Football has brought me more pleasure and excitement, perhaps, than any other of my interests. Often, on my own, or in the company of other football addicts, I relive that magical day in April 1965 when Kilmarnock won the Scottish 1st Division Championship. Those were the days when the 1st Division Championship was the supreme honour in Scottish football. With depressing regularity, the Championship had became monopolised by the big teams, especially the famous 'Old Firm' pair, Rangers and Celtic.

Kilmarnock came to Tynecastle on that April Saturday in 1965 to play what was to be the greatest game in their history. For both teams, it was the last game of the season. Hearts, with 50 points, needed only a draw to take the Championship. Kilmarnock, with 48 points and inferior goal average, had to win by at least 2-0 to gain the honour.

By the middle of the second half, goals by Dave Sneddon and Brian McIlroy had given Kilmarnock the lead they needed. Needing only to score one goal, Hearts besieged the Kilmarnock goal; tension grew to unbelievable proportions in the 35,000 crowd as the minutes ticked away. Bobby Ferguson's goalkeeping skill cast a spell upon Hearts which they never managed to break.

Extraordinary scenes greeted the final whistle. All round the ground, the stand included, Kilmarnock fans shook hands with each other, babbled to each other, congratulated each other: hats, bonnets and scarves went up in the air. Many a tear was wiped away.

On to the field rushed hundreds of Kilmarnock supporters. With great good sense, the Edinburgh Police did not intervene as the players were surrounded, shaken by the hand, embraced, pummelled and lifted shoulder high. Almost first among the invaders was Kilmarnock manager Willie Waddell who made a bee-line for the team captain, Frank Beattie, and lifted him high in triumphant salute.

My eyes were moist as I looked down on the scene from the Tynecastle press box. Momentarily, in the midst of the excitement, the thought occurred to me that I might have witnessed the last time Scotland will see a town team win the top League Championship. In front of me, in the stand, six or seven rows from the back, I could see one of Kilmarnock's staunchest supporters, Provost Danny Cairns.

"Well done, boys," he was calling "Well done, boys. You've done us a' proud."

The Provost's pleasure was not shared by everyone in the stand. Two rows behind him, a Hearts supporter called to him to sit down. "I canna see the field," said the Hearts man. "You're blockin' my view. Sit on your backside."

Turning round, the Provost pointed a forefinger. "See, here, son," he said. "See you here. I've waited over sixty years for this day... and I'm no' sittin' doon for you or anybody else. I wouldn't sit down for the Queen today, let alone you."

I have a special reason for remembering another showdown with Hearts. On 27th October, 1962, Kilmarnock lost 1-0 to Hearts in the League Cup Final at Hampden. Normally, defeat never depresses me, since I have always used yesterday's defeat to enhance the pleasure of today's victory. But, as I looked round the Hampden bowl with its 60,000 spectators, I strayed in imagination to the seas north of Cuba. That afternoon, I knew, Russian ships carrying nuclear missiles to Cuba were fast approaching an American fleet blockading the northern approaches to the island. Hearts were doing a lap of honour by this time, and I wondered what would happen if the immovable object and the irresistible force were at last to meet in the Atlantic.

On the way home, I heard on the car radio that the Russians had turned back their ships. I almost forgave referee Tiny Wharton for ruling that Frank Beattie's last-minute 'equaliser' had been scored with his hand and not his head. You can never rely on the witness of a dim-sighted referee who turns up without his contact lenses.

HUNGER MARCH AND STRIKE

Along with the rest of the country, Kilmarnock greeted the end of the Great War of 1914-18 with the joyful sounds of thanksgiving. The slaughter had stopped, the world was at peace again, a brave new world lay ahead.

As quiet settled at last on the Western Front, Kilmarnock celebrated, but only for a brief moment. Soldiers returned to find there wasn't enough work for them all, and very likely none at all if they happened to be disabled by war wounds.

Slowly and painfully, Kilmarnock dragged itself into the 1920s. To the credit of the Town Council, new houses began to make their appearance in good numbers thanks to the financial assistance given under post-war housing legislation. But the new bricks and mortar could do no more than patch the decaying mass of local housing. Living conditions, which had deteriorated during the war, continued to deteriorate. Unemployment brought poverty, hunger and disease. World depression had set in and was to last until the nations got involved in war again in 1939.

Queues at the Labour Exchange in Morton Place grew longer and longer. Those who managed to find a trade were sacked as soon as their time was out. All too often, the hunt for new work took Kilmarnock men to England. Introduction of the Means Test in 1932 made living conditions worse by stopping unemployment benefit at the end of six months. Not much was left for great numbers of people except a breadline existence and parish relief. England continued to take Scotland's unemployed. But the greatest exodus was to Canada and America.

Destitution was far from uncommon. Voluntary organisations manned soup kitchens, and those who couldn't afford a copper or two to get shelter in a lodging house had no alternative but to sleep rough. Pawnshops and second-hand shops were busy. The Salvation Army worked ceaselessly to allay the plight of those who were unable to cope. The Co-operative became the quartermaster for Kilmarnock, feeding and clothing non-members as well as members with no thought of profit, rather a desire and need to help.

In 1922, disappointment with the failure of Government to make life more tolerable for the mass of people inspired another of those mass demonstrations against injustice which had been common in Chartist times.

On 1st December, 1922, a contingent of 400 unemployed Glasgow men (Hunger Marchers they were called) marched into Kilmarnock, banners flying, on their way to London. The plan was to join Hunger Marchers from other parts of Britain in a demonstration which would persuade the Prime Minister, Mr. Bonar Law, to use the power of Government to take the misery and uncertainty out of the lives of working people.

The Glasgow Hunger Marchers were fed in the Labour Room and stayed overnight in the Art Gallery. When they resumed their journey, the marchers said they hoped to reach London by the 22nd of December.

If it did nothing else, the Hunger Marchers forced Britain to look at itself and consider the injustice which was being meted out to the country's workers.

Dissatisfaction expressed itself again in 1926. For ten days, the country was paralysed by a general strike. When the strike was called off by the Trades Union Congress on 12th May, strikers in Kilmarnock refused at first to believe the news. Hundreds who had gathered in Portland Street, refused to allow the Scottish Transport Company buses to leave the station.

Rumours later got around Kilmarnock that all the demands made by the TUC had been granted. A meeting was wrongly told that the strike had achieved victory.

Confirmation that the strike had been called off by the TUC came in a BBC wireless bulletin that night. The strike was definitely over in Kilmarnock, and, except for the miners, who held out on their own for months, it was over for the rest of Britain as well.

SANDY WALKED BACKWARDS TO EDINBURGH

Sandy Mackie who died at his home in Robertson Place, Kilmarnock, in 1937, enjoys a special place in local history because of two epic journeys he made in the early 1920s.

Blessed with outstanding ability as a runner, Sandy made a point of running in as many athletics meetings in

Ayrshire as he could. Accompanying him as a sort of trainer-medic, his mother, 'Old Ann,' administered any assistance he needed.

Sandy was outstanding over the quarter-mile, even better over 100 yards. At this latter distance, he could break the tape in just over 10 seconds. Not surprisingly, he won many prizes on the track.

Sandy's ability as a runner brought him fame well beyond Kilmarnock. Finding himself arguing about athletics in Pie Reid's pub, Sandy rashly bet that he could walk to Edinburgh as fast as anyone—"Backwards, tied to a pram," he added.

And that is exactly what Sandy did. One Saturday morning, in the presence of a great crowd, Sandy left for Edinburgh, backwards, harnessed to a pram. To ensure his safety, he was preceded by his friend Tucker Mc-Cluckie.

The wager was won. Sandy made the journey to and from Edinburgh backwards, and tied to a pram. Not long afterwards, he walked to London and back in very good time, without the pram this time.

Brought up in Kilmaurs, Sandy went into the mines when only 10 or 11 years old. He was a fine drummer and, during the miners strike of 1894, his mates in Ballochmyle Colliery could always depend on Sandy Mackie and the band he had gathered round him to keep their spirits up.

During the 1914-18 war, Sandy showed another aspect of the musician in him. The soldiers who guarded Ballochmyle Bridge were often entertained by the skirl of his pipes.

Coal-hewer, staunch comrade, eccentric, athlete, musician, even pugilist—Sandy Mackie, though not born in Kilmarnock, added much to its character and colour.

THE FIRST ALL-ELECTRIC HOUSE

Most people in Kilmarnock must have thought they were dreaming when the town's first all-electric Corporation house was opened in Middleton Park in September 1922. Only three years earlier, they had welcomed the completion of the first ordinary, 'no frills' corporation house.

The Middleton Park house was packed with electric gadgetry, still not affordable today by huge numbers of people. The thousands who looked over the house after it had been opened by Lady Walker enjoyed pushing buttons and switches to cook, boil, heat, clean, sweep, iron and illuminate. There was even, yes, an electric dishwasher on show.

An imaginative show by the Town Council, one which also showed the electrical manufacturing industry geared to equip the houses with devices to remove the drudgery of housework. But, think of the effect on the hundreds within half-a-mile of Middleton Park, still bringing up families in houses decaying round their ears. Some of them would have been much happier, and more comfortable, had they been provided with an inside water tap and w.c.

THE TRAGEDY OF TOWNHOLM

Influenced by the mood of optimism which spread over the country when the Great War ended in 1919, Kilmarnock Town Council had been quick to use the subsidies and cheap capital offered under the new Housing Acts. No time was lost by Kilmarnock in helping the Prime Minister, Mr. David Lloyd George, to transform Britain into "a fit Britain for heroes to live in."

Attractive houses soon sprang up in Scott Road, Holehouse Road, and Longpark, all of brick construction. There was no evident shortage of cash, as was borne out later by the appearance of more and more new housing estates. And yet, in 1924, when Corporation houses were being built by the score, the Council decided to purchase Army surplus tin huts and to erect them at Townholm, as accommodation for displaced slum tenants.

There was no denying the need to provide a more civilized environment for the tenants from the slum area of Fore street. Vermin bred unchecked, disease was rampant and, at one stage, infantile mortality was running at 130 deaths for every 1000 live births. The neighbourhood had decayed almost to the point of death. New homes were certainly needed, and long overdue. But why purchase ten rusty tin huts when there were new brick houses waiting for new tenants?

Immediately the tin huts appeared in Townholm, the district was dubbed Tin Town or Shanty Town. The prestige and dignity enjoyed by other districts of the town were denied to it.

Tenants who came to occupy the 160 brick houses eventually built at Townholm found themselves increasingly isolated. Finding new tenants for houses as they became vacant was never easy. The search became even more difficult when talk got around that Townholm was being used as a reception centre for anti-social tenants.

Against this unhappy background, Townholm's housing stock steadily declined, as did community relations. When Kilmarnock Town Council tried to introduce standard rents for the same accommodation throughout the town in the 1960s, the tenants of Townholm refused to pay any increase in rent. ' No increase in rent unless we get better houses and amenities,' they said. To make their point, the tenants mounted a protest march on the Town Hall. The council admitted the justice of the rebel cause and cancelled the rent increases.

Townholm has now been abandoned as a housing estate. Today, it lies bare and empty, waiting, with reasonable hope, to be given the dignified place it deserves in local history, perhaps as part of Dean Castle Country Park.

SAILING DOWN THE RIVER

There was a wonderful time in the early 1930s when the River Irvine did much better for Kilmarnock than carry the sewage of the four Irvine Valley towns to the Firth of

Clyde. For a few well-remembered years, the people of Kilmarnock were able to enjoy the pleasures of boating on the Irvine.

Behind this imaginative enterprise was a man called Jack Robertson who lived with his wife and family in New Mill Road.

A painter to trade, Mr. Robertson bought a couple of single sculls or skiffs, two double sculls, and a flat-bottom rowing boat. A thorough clean-up, a coat of paint and varnish by Mr. Robertson himself, and his fleet was ready for hire.

Harbour was a quiet spot where the Samson Avenue Burn joined the River Irvine, very near to the New Mill. Here, Mr. Robertson moored his boats, put up a sign 'Boats for hire' and quietly awaited public response.

Kilmarnock in the 1930s hadn't yet developed the habit of punting down the Grand Canal, or sailing out from the marinas of the Cote d'azur (unemployment and the Means Test were successfully delaying these holiday pleasures) so there was immediate interest in the Robertson fleet.

When the weather was good, the boats were seldom at their moorings except to embark and disembark rowers and passengers.

To hire a single boat, a skiff, for an hour cost about a shilling. You could share a two-seater with a pal for 9d each. To go cruising in the flat-bottom cost 3d per person, and a sworn undertaking that you would take your turn at the oars.

The hardiest and the wealthiest preferred to hire the single skiffs and engage in a man-versus-water act which they hoped would go down well with the local talent. If you and your pal were still talking, you got your wind out in a session of double-sculling along a mile-and-a-half of water from the Red Brig at Struthers Steps to the Glenfield Bridge at Riccarton.

As business prospered, Mr. Robertson launched a motor boat on the river. The *Nancy Stair,* as it was called, proved successful with mothers and weans. With Mr. Robertson at the helm, the *Nancy Stair* chugged its dignified way downstream, greeted by waves and cheers from the residents of Victoria Terrace and Riverbank Terrace. After a ponderous turn in sight of the Glenfield, the *Nancy* chugged even more slowly upstream past her moorings and into the far-eastern reaches of the Irvine. Popular acclaim was once again bestowed upon the mariners, coming this time from the crowds of boys who had plunged in from the Carra and Irvy entry points on the embankment.

The boats were long gone by the time war started in 1939. How pleasant it would be for Kilmarnock to see them back, now that the sewage from the four Irvine Valley towns goes down to the sea in pipes, and the salmon has ventured back to the upper reaches of the water.

About the same time as Mr. Robertson's fleet was sailing, it was common practice in the winter to skate on the river. But, those were the days when winter could be depended upon to bring ice for skating and curling.

Burns Monument, Kay Park, opened 1879
Monument designed by Mr. Ingram, Kilmarnock
Marble statue executed by Mr. W.G. Stevenson, Edinburgh

MONKEY BUSINESS AT BURNS MONUMENT

Befitting its place as home of the Burns Federation, Kilmarnock in 1958 was putting great care and imagination into preparations for the world-wide celebration of the bicentenary of the birth of the Bard on 25th January the following year, 1959.

Hundreds of Burnsians joined in the preparation of a salute which would reflect the greatness of the occasion and the special relationship between Burns and Kilmarnock. Genial summer weather helped the work pleasantly along. All was well with the Burnsian world.

But, as the Bard has often told us, the best-laid schemes o' mice and men gang aft agley. On to the stage came an American professor of Literature by the name of J.W. Egerer. All at once, quiet gave way to uproar.

A world-famous authority on Burns, Professor Egerer had come to Scotland in search of bibliography which he was compiling on the poet's life. His tour of the Burns Country ended at the Kay Park Museum in Kilmarnock. There, in the shadow of the famous statue of the poet, Professor Egerer had an experience he was long to remember–and Kilmarnock and the Federation as well.

In a letter to Mr. J.F.T. Thomson, the then Curator of the Dick Institute, Professor Egerer complained that valuable manuscripts and books were not being properly cared for. The museum was in a shocking state, he said.

Later, when his criticism had hit the headlines in the national press, Professor Egerer said he had been particularly shocked to find walls covered in graffiti, and a glass panel covering a portrait of the poet smeared in lipstick with the words, "I love Tommy Steele." Most incredible discovery of all, said Professor Egerer, was that the Museum had become the home for a Monkey Band, a Victorian children's toy.

It was an occasion in Kilmarnock and the Burns Movement, when, had times been less civilised, there would have been public hangings at the Cross.

The Monkey Band was identified as a savings bank which had once belonged to a prominent local businessman. Put a penny in the slot, and two monkeys said a noisy thankyou by banging cymbals together. Official explanation of its presence was that it encouraged children to visit the museum.

Children's attraction or no, the Monkey Band was quickly found another concert platform. Some of the documents and books were taken away for remedial treatment, and those that were left were given adequate protection. The walls and panels were stripped of graffiti and lipstick.

By the time 25th January, 1959, arrived, the famous Kay Park Monument was in wholesome state, fit to receive the world in its 200th annual homage to the Bard. Thanks to the chance visit of an American Professor of Literature, the Monument has never been the same since.

WHITHER CORPORATION HOUSING?

Replacement of slums by attractive new houses has been one of the great achievements of local authorities since the end of the Great War of 1914-18.

In common with other local authorities, Kilmarnock has made full use of the housing subsidies provided by Act of Parliament from 1919. Between 1919 and the start of the 1939-1945 war, over 1,800 corporation houses were built in districts such as Holehouse Road, Scott Road, Townholm, Bonnyton, Ayr Road, New Mill Road, Riccarton, London Road, Longpark, Knockinlaw and Hillhead.

As the new houses went up, the old ones came down. The result was a healthier, happier environment for the townspeople, better and improving prospects of new houses for young couples planning to get married, and for couples living in sub-lets and sub-standard accommodation.

As soon as war ended in 1945, Kilmarnock Town Council resumed its vigorous programme of slum clearance and rehousing. With continuing assistance from Government, thousands of new homes were provided, most of them in the outskirts of the town–Burnpark and Witchknowe, Shortlees, Bellfield, Onthank, New Farm Loch. Cleared sites in the town itself were re-stocked with good houses. As far as could be done, people in greatest need were supplied first.

Flats, cottages, and maisonettes in a variety of designs and size catered in the main for the homeless and those in sub-lets.

Older people were accommodated, whenever possible, in the centre of the town. Those who needed assistance to stay in their own homes found it in supervised hostels and sheltered accommodation. Single persons, unmarried couples, single-parent families were given their share of the housing harvest. By the 1960s, housing waiting lists were being eaten into. The situation encouraged the Town Council to introduce central heating in new houses as they were built. A programme for fitting older houses with central heating was introduced about five years ago.

Constant though housing progress has been in Kilmarnock since 1919, the local authority began to find about 1980 that their housing stock was deteriorating, particularly in certain areas of the town. Reduction in housing subsidy made repairs increasingly difficult, people on the waiting list were becoming choosier. On top of this, there was a growing market for private housing. Construction of much-needed new council houses slowed down.

Today, local authorities are required to sell off their housing stocks at prices fixed by district valuers. Since Kilmarnock and Loudoun District Council (successors to Kilmarnock Town Council in 1975) sold their first corporation house in July 1981, sales from their stock of over 10,000 houses had risen to 2,366 by April of this year. The Scottish Special Housing Association is also having to sell off its housing stock. Cost of replacing a standard 4-apartment house is estimated at £26,000.

Faced with a growing waiting list (2,284 in March of this year compared with 2,001 in April 1977), the District Council joined up with Barratt's and Portland Developments in restoring 179 houses which were in a serious state of decline in Knockinlaw. The Knockinlaw Project, as the scheme was called, required the District Council to sell off 126 houses to Barratt's and 9 to Portland Developments.

What the future holds for local-authority housing is uncertain. In the past ten years, the District Council has built only 95 houses.

Reduction in council housing is being offset, to some extent, by an increase in private building. Attractive estates have sprung up in various parts of the town, and there is a ready market for the houses. Private builders and developers are also adding to the growing number of owner-occupiers by restoring old housing property. Here again, buyers are found in plenty.

THEATRE, OPERA HOUSE, AND CINEMA

Kilmarnock's contribution to the fascinating world of entertainment began just before the start of last century.

The town's first theatre was a converted suite of stables which stood on ground behind what is now British Home Stores in King Street. There, the town's first first-nighters could see Edmund Kean, probably Britain's foremost actor of the day, in one of his great Shakespearean roles, heightened, when the air began to warm up, by a pleasant aroma of the countryside. Gustavus Brooks, another fine actor, gave his first performance on this stage when only a boy.

The old theatre remained open until it was bought by the Commercial Bank in 1855. Among the last performances was a private recital by Paganini, the Italian violin virtuoso and composer.

The Opera House, opened in John Finnie Street in 1875, had a varied career. By the late 1920s, the Opera House had changed its role and become St. John's U.F. Church. Later, it changed its mantle again and became an auction saleroom. Earlier this year (1989), the Opera House, then in its fourth existence as a public house, was destroyed by fire.

Between 1900 and outbreak of the Great War in 1914, Kilmarnock became caught up, along with the rest of the country, in the celluloid tentacles reaching out from the vast Hollywood film studios. Music-hall, revue, stage comedy and drama continued to be offered in the Palace Theatre, opened in 1903, and in the King's Theatre, opened in 1904. But, before war broke out in 1914, both the Palace and the Kings were being forced to double up as picturehouses.

Kilmarnock's first picturehouse was probably the Electric, converted out of Clerk's Lane Church. It opened in 1911 and lasted until it was demolished in 1938 to make way for a car park.

Between the end of the Great War in 1918 and the start of the next war in 1939, Kilmarnock brought its total of picturehouses, cinemas as they were now being called, to seven . The Scotia, the first of that name in Scotland, opened up in Union Street in 1920. Twice it was to change its name, first to the Savoy, finally to the Imperial, and it ended its days as a dance hall. The final public performance in the Imperial came in the 1950s, members of the public filing in to see, and hear, a musician called Syncopating Sandy attack what was billed as an attempt on the world record for continuous piano–playing. Sandy broke the record, and came close to breaking himself as a result. He was a sorry sight at the close of his performance.

The Forum Picturehouse, which stood on the site now occupied by Fine Fare Supermarket in Titchfield Street, opened for business about the same time as the Scotia. In 1923 came the George Picturehouse, converted from the George Hotel. It ended life as a bingo hall: the building is still in use as shopping accommodation.

The last cinema to be built in Kilmarnock was the Plaza, opened in 1940. When it closed in 1971 to make way for road improvements and the construction of Marks and Spencer's, Kilmarnock's cinemas, seven in number in their heyday, were reduced to only one, the King's.

Opened in 1904, the King's provided a platform for many famous artistes, among them Sir Harry Lauder, Harry Gordon and Fred Karno. In 1934, to meet the change from Theatre to Cinema, it changed its style to the Regal Cinema. But, before the change, it introduced 'the talkies' to Kilmarnock in 1929. Today, the King's Theatre, later the Regal Cinema, is still with us as the ABC (3 in 1) Cinema, the last picturehouse in Kilmarnock.

The Palace Theatre is also still in use. After a long and vulnerable existence as theatre and cinema, the Palace is enjoying some success as a civic theatre.

EARLY VIEWS OF KILMARNOCK — The two scenes shown on this page are from etchings based on paintings by David Octavius Hill. The paintings were commissioned from D.O. Hill to provide illustration for John Wilson's book *The Land of Burns* and were produced between 1834 and 1840. The book proved very popular and was reprinted several times. The scene above is of Kilmarnock viewed from the vicinity of Riccarton, with the town framed by the local parish church on the right and a farmhouse on the left. The etching this is taken from was by W. Richardson. The scene below is one of the oldest prints of Kilmarnock Cross, and was etched by J. Wilson. The skyline is dominated by the Laigh Kirk on the right, the tower and steeple of the Council House on the left and King Street church steeple in the middle. Youngest of the three buildings, King-Street church was opened in 1832 almost 30 years after the formation of King Street. The original painting of the cross can often be viewed at the Dick Institute, where it is a popular exhibit.

BORLAND WATER AND DEAN QUARRY — Borland Water and Dean Quarry in 1859. It was stone from this quarry which was used by Lord Howard de Walden to restore Dean Castle, destroyed by fire in 1735. The photograph reproduced here was taken by Alan McGregor who had a photographic studio at Robertson Land, King Street, Kilmarnock. The studio was in business from the middle of the 19th century until around 1912.

KING STREET, EARLY 19th CENTURY — An old print showing where Johnnie Walker's world-famous whisky-blending business started in 1820 as a "small Italian warehouse, grocery and wine and spirit business." (Kilmarnock Standard, September 1956). The remarkable success of 'Johnnie Walker' whisky led to establishment of the firm's first bonded warehouse in Croft Street in 1873. Six years later, cottages in Strand Street were demolished to make way for extension of the bond and the addition of a bottling warehouse and offices.

JOHN FINNIE STREET, EARLY 19th CENTURY — A view of John Finnie Street shortly after its opening in 1864.

SOUTH GATEHOUSE, BELLFIELD ESTATE — A milk cart, as used by farmers for vending milk to customers, very common in the streets of Kilmarnock and elsewhere in Scotland in the latter part of last century and well into the present one. One of the luggies contains sweet milk, the other sour. A draw-off tap on the back of the luggies allowed the farmer to empty the required amount of milk into measuring cans, usually of pint or half-pint size, which hung handily beside the taps. There is a step fixed to the rear shaft, used by the driver, for stepping down from and stepping back into the cart.

KILMARNOCK CROSS LOOKING NORTH, circa 1880 — In the centre is the Town Well. During the 16th century, the thatched building contained a shop owned by a Mr. Jasper Tough. Surviving the massacre of French Huguenots in Paris on St. Bartholomew's day 1572, Mr. Tough fled to Scotland. It was out of the frying pan and into the fire for him. His sympathies for the Covenanters and his insistence on giving medical aid to their supporters resulted in frequent fines; on one occasion he was jailed, on another his worldly possessions were seized.

JOHN FINNNIE STREET, circa 1880 — The suite of buildings on the right houses the Oddfellows Hall. The Independent Order of Odd Fellows was a benevolent institution organised on a system similar to the masons. The Kilmarnock Lodge was founded in 1841 and, by the start of the present century, it had an adult membership of 1,200 and a strong juvenile membership.

RICCARTON POST OFFICE, circa 1900 — The 'VR' (Victoria Regina) atop the letter box on the right helps to place the photograph about the turn of the century. Mrs. Shedden, standing in the doorway wearing her mutch, crocheted shawl and apron, looks just the person to sell you some Sunlight Soap, gooseberry jelly, Van Houten's Cocoa, fresh farm eggs, matches or soor plooms. In addition to selling stamps, accepting letters or parcels for posting and marking up Post Office Savings Bank pass books, the post office could also send a message over the wires by the magic of the telegraph.

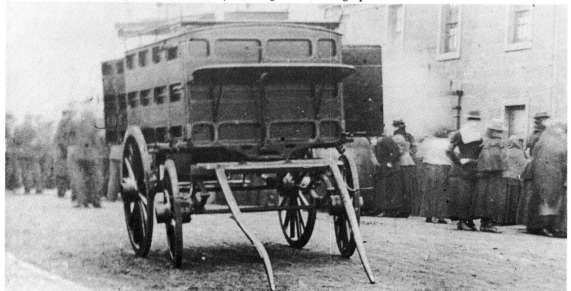

FIRE FIGHTING, 100 YEARS AGO — A nineteenth century predecessor of the modern fire tender. In all probability, this wagon, pictured about 1880, was modelled on the "water machine for extinguishing fires", purchased for £40 by the Town Council in 1753. With the water machine went 40 feet of leather hose pipe which pumped water from an on-board tank and projected it on to the fire. When the wagon in our picture reached its destination, the horse was taken from the shafts and tethered at a safe distance. The firemen were then free to go about their business.

CURLING AT NEW FARM LOCH, c. 1895 — The Loch, which was filled in November and drained out at the end of March, covered several acres and provided a venue for curlers for over a century from 1845. Curling was also played at the Kilmarnock Water below the Black Rocks, Kay Park, and on artificial ponds at London Road and Bellfield. The Statistical Account of 1845 gives the number of curlers in Kilmarnock as 300. There were 4 clubs in the town when curling was at the height of its popularity — Townhead (the first), Kilmarnock Senior, Kilmarnock Junior and Kilmarnock Union. By 1938, only Townhead remained. The curler in the centre is wearing the cloth or carpet boot, preferred by local curlers to the metal crampit which cut up the ice badly.

KING STREET IN THE 1890's — Looking up King Street towards the Cross on a bright sunny day. It is hot enough for the shopkeepers to let their shades down. The youngsters are shading their eyes from the sun while watching the photographer go about his work.

FUNERAL PROCESSION, circa 1900 — A funeral makes its way through the Cross and along Duke Street to the cemetery in Grassyards Road. It was the practice on such occasions for pedestrians to stand to attention as the hearse passed and for men to doff their headgear as a mark of respect.

KILMARNOCK ATHLETIC ANCIENTS — Pictured in Howard Park are footballers of Kilmarnock Athletic Ancients of the 1890s. With one exception, all the players are sporting moustaches. The heavy pigskin boots were the cause of many serious injuries and good reason for wearing bulky leg guards for protection.

RICCARTON TOLL-HOUSE — A relic of the days of the turnpike roads of the late 19th century. This is the toll-house at Riccarton where tolls were paid by travellers proceeding to Ayr. Traffic was stopped by a turnpike covering the entire width of the road.

KILMARNOCK MINERS, circa 1880 — "I belong to the breed of hardy, mongrel creatures whose menfolk have burrowed like rats in the black bowels of the earth for generations in quest of coal. I am a miner, the son of a miner, the grandson of a miner, the great-grandson of a miner. As a child, I have hearkened to stories of pits and pitmen, stories of disaster, of death, and of heroism, stories of strikes, coercion, intimidation, and victimisation, stories of want, suffering, and sin." Any one of the miners in this photograph could have been the one quoted in the mining feature of the Third Statistical Account of Scotland (Ayrshire Section). All of them, in fact, are Kilmarnock miners, about to enter the cage and descend to the coal-face for another day's back-breaking toil. The two boys at the front would be no more than 10 years old, and should have been at school, but, because their parents needed their wages, they had been granted a dispensation to work down the pit.

JOHN FINNIE STREET, circa 1900 — John Finnie Street about the start of the present century. The central premises of Kilmarnock Co-operative Society, formed in 1860, are seen bottom right. First-floor of building in bottom-left housed 'the Club', a meeting place for local businessmen.

KILMARNOCK CROSS, circa 1900 — On the right stands what was called a Badge Porter's Barrow. The porter was an employee of the railway company, invested with the sole right of carrying goods to and from the railway station. Symbol of this monopoly was the porter's badge. Behind the statue of Jimmy Shaw can be seen Rankin's wine and whisky shop, going strong when Johnnie Walker's was founded in 1820. On the left, another old family business — Lauder the hatter's.

WEST LANGLANDS STREET, circa 1890 — The lorry parked outside the warehouses is emblazoned with the sign "Bargains" and looks very like an early type of travelling shop, the driver doubling up as salesman at the open sides of the vehicle.

KILMARNOCK MERCHANTS CYCLING CLUB — Before the First World War, pedal power was the new-fangled craze. Here we see a few of the velocipede's devotees. Kilmarnock Merchants Cycling Club (see A Pioneering Bicyclist).

SLAUGHTERHOUSE STAFF, circa 1900 — The staff of Kilmarnock Corporation Slaughterhouse in St. Andrew's Street, 1900 - 1905. Following a large increase in houses built in this area, the decision was taken to close this slaughterhouse and erect a new one on the banks of the Kilmarnock Water, near its junction with the River Irvine.

Included in the picture are:— J. Ross, G. Cleary Jun., W. Wallace, J. Smith, W. Alexander, J. Connell, J. McCairtney, J. White, M. Caldwell, C. Greenshields, J. McLaren, C. Johnstone, P. Johnstone, G. Cleary, D. Nicol.

FLITTING — Taken in Langlands Street, this photo shows one family's problem of trying to load their wordly possessions on to a wagon no more than 15 feet by 8 feet. The loose straw has probably come from the mattress, or tike, as it was known locally. Very few working-class people could afford to buy a feather bed or even one stuffed with flock. Their beds were usually stuffed with straw, like army palliasses.

HOWARD PARK — Play area of the Howard Park or Barbadoes Green, as it was called when gifted to Kilmarnock by Baroness Howard de Walden. Originally, this ground was laid out as a football pitch, one of two pitches in the Park. The clubhouse can be seen on the right; in the background, the Saxone Shoe factory advertises itself.

KAY PARK FOUNTAIN, circa 1902 — The fountain and bandstand dominate the foreground of this picture while the Burns Monument towers over the scene. A favourite Sunday venue for Kilmarnock people, who would picnic round the fountain and enjoy the sound of the 'Burra Baun'. Many a wean was lifted drookit from the fountain as a result of over-exuberant fun with friends.

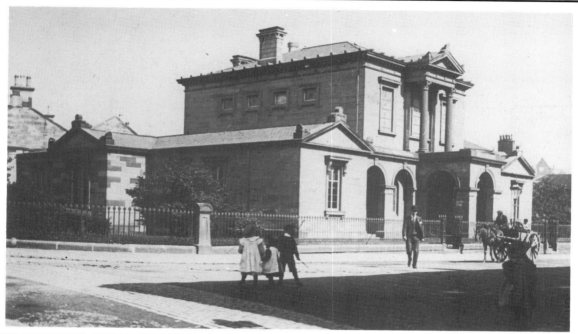

KILMARNOCK SHERIFF COURT HOUSE, circa 1900 — Built in 1852, just six years after the appointment of Kilmarnock's first residential Sheriff-Substitute, the Court House continued in use until the opening of the new Court House in 1986, on a site opposite.

KILMARNOCK SHERIFF COURT HOUSE, 1989 — Now that the new Sheriff Court House on the corner of St. Marnock Street and Dundonald Road is in use, sittings of the High Court are held there. The fabric of the old Court House is being restored and now contains the Procurator Fiscal's office.

KILMARNOCK CROSS — Jimmy Shaw watches in approving silence while the citizens of Kilmarnock enjoy a leisurely summer day. A horse drawing a lorry loaded with bales of wool heads down Portland Street towards the Cross.

KING STREET, 1901 — Looking towards the Cross, the Townhouse, or Council Chamber, dominates the sky-line. It was built in 1801 and demolished in the 1970s to make way for redevelopment of the town centre. On the right beyond the street lamp is the Royal Bank, beyond that Lauder the baker's and Lewis's, the furniture and jewellery store.

MAMALEE — Two of the town's many 'Johnny a' things,' shops which contrived to sell almost everything you could reasonably need. In the centre of the picture is Mamalee, the first black man to be seen in Kilmarnock. Servant to a Kilmarnock man in the Far East, Mamalee came to Kilmarnock when his master died. Though well cared for and well liked by the people of Kilmarnock, Scotland's climate was too harsh for Mamalee and he did not live long after coming here.

GREENLEES AND SONS — Greenlees boot and shoe shop in King Street, possibly before the First World War. Note the cavalry boot sign and the fussy gas wall lamp. Typical of the window-dressing practice of the day, the shop has hardly a square inch of free space round door and window.

KILMARNOCK'S FIRST ELECTRIC TRAMCAR, 1904 — This was the first electric tramcar to run in Kilmarnock. The day before the public service began in December, 1904, the system was given a thorough check by Board of Trade inspectors. Our photograph shows the inspectors at the car shed in Greenholm Street about to begin their tour of inspection in Car No. 8. On the following day, 10th December, Lord Howard de Walden set the public tramways system going.

THE HORSELESS CARRIAGE, circa 1900 — The window of R. & J.F. Dunlop advertises popular makes of bicycle — Singer, Royal Enfield and James — and at the same time locates the scene as High Glencairn Street. The car would have been one of the first to be seen in Kilmarnock and, judging from its new solid tyres and shiny carbide (acetylene) lamps, is straight off the production line. The acetylene gas burnt in the lamps was given off by the chemical reaction of water on calcium carbide.

PASSENGER-CARRYING MOTOR WAGONETTE, circa 1900 — One of the first passenger-carrying motor wagonettes in Kilmarnock. This one plied between the town and Fenwick. The chain drive to the rear wheels and the outside brake cable are clearly visible.

THE LONG PULL, 1903 — Today, Barclay locomotives travel along their own track to the railway sidings for despatch to customers. But, in 1903, things were vastly different. Finished locomotives were hauled from the workshops on to the roadway by manpower. Here we see Barclay workers about to start the long pull along Langlands Street to the sidings, an operation which damaged the road surface. The puff of smoke from the chimney of the locomotive suggests the driver is helping in the haul with a little steam power.

THE GEORGE HOTEL — Built in the early part of last century, the George Hotel stood on the corner of Portland Street and West George Street. The George was Kilmarnock's '5-star hotel'. This was where visiting VIPs stayed and were feted and where important public functions were held. Andrew Fisher, Crosshouse-born Prime Minister of Australia, was guest of honour here at a dinner during which the Town Council conferred the Freedom of Kilmarnock on him. The George Hotel closed down in 1920, and, in that same year, part of the building was adapted for use as the George Cinema.

WEST GEORGE STREET, circa 1900 — On the left, at the junction of John Finnie Street, West George Street and Garden Street, a horse stands yoked to a platform lorry. The iron-tyred wheels of the lorry make it difficult for the horse to pull the lorry uphill to the railway station. Help is needed from the trace horse, seen here emerging from Garden Street. Together, they will get the lorry to the Station for loading. A local train can be seen on the viaduct, possibly on its way to the towns of the Irvine Valley.

DUNDONALD ROAD, 1905 — Taken from near Howard Park looking towards John Finnie Street, this picture shows a combination of gas and electric street lighting.

LAUDER BRIDGE, 1905 — This is the scene a few minutes after Mrs Margaret Lauder opened a new suspension bridge over the Kilmarnock Water at Dean Ford, near the Dark Path, in June 1905. Built for £170 from public subscriptions raised by Mrs Lauder's husband, Hugh, the bridge had a span of 90 feet and a walkway just under 4 feet wide. So many people rushed on to the bridge, after the ribbon was cut, that it subsided gently into the water. Fortunately no-one was injured and the bridge was soon replaced. It came to be known as the Swinging Bridge because of the gentle movement which it sometimes made in the wind.

COLLEGE WYND, circa 1900 — It is believed that the street name was derived from the site of an old educational institution located here. The empty tea box at the edge of the pavement was probably used as a rubbish receptacle and is awaiting the corporation cleansing cart.

COLLEGE WYND, 1989 — The modern face of College Wynd, one of the oldest parts of Kilmarnock. The 'cosmetics' of mortar and roughcast have given the old properties on the left a facelift which should see them well into the next century. At the top of the Wynd is the building which now serves as Civic Centre for Kilmarnock and Loudoun District Council. On the right, the Wynd touches the hallowed ground of Laigh Kirkyard.

JOCK FISHER, COALMAN — Nobody was better known within a half-mile radius of his home and business in Robertson Place than Jock Fisher, the coalman. Jock was in partnership with his brother Rab and sister Mary. Mary always seemed to be at the counter of her store selling paraffin, candles, kindling sticks, turpentine, matches and black soap. Jock worked his round from Monday to Saturday, selling coal mostly in 'quarters' i.e. a quarter of a hundred-weight or 28lbs, the maximum amount the scales, seen here dangling at the back of his cart, could weigh.

THE STRAND — The group of men and children are from families living in Dunlop Street, on the left. To the right, the opening to Croft Street can be seen. From this point to the top of the steps leading to West George Street was the home for many years of the Kilmarnock Barras, something to look forward to on Saturday nights. At the corner of Croft Street and the Strand was Johnnie Walker's bonded warehouse and in the Strand itself the cooperage.

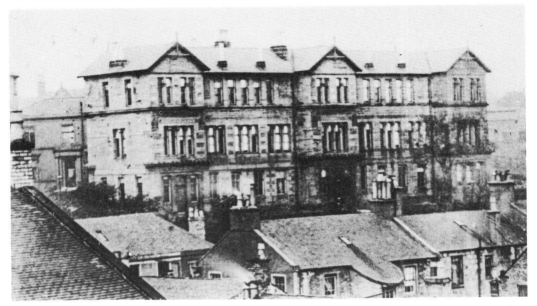

KILMARNOCK INFIRMARY — To meet the needs of Kilmarnock's growing population, Kilmarnock Infirmary was opened in 1869 at the northern end of Portland Street. Originally an infectious-diseases hospital as well as one providing medical and surgical services, the Infirmary was immediately in business dealing with illness and disease, the results of accidents in factory and pit. In the year of opening, 1869, the Infirmary dealt with 101 cases. Ten years later, the number of cases had risen to 420. By 1907, the number had more than trebled to 1,289. Opening of Kirklandside Infectious Diseases Hospital relieved pressure on the Infirmary and allowed it to play the roll of general hospital for the rest of its time. Kilmarnock workers had full and free access to the Infirmary through the Workers Contributary Scheme right up to the start of the National Health Service in 1948.

CROSSHOUSE GENERAL HOSPITAL — Today Kilmarnock Infirmary has been succeeded by Crosshouse General Hospital, opened in 1982.

THE CROSS AND KING STREET — Taken around 1910, the double tram track linking Beansburn and Riccarton is completely free of tram-cars. On the left is the town's first underground lavatory, heavily protected by iron railings. One of the two gentlemen on the left leans thoughtfully on the iron wondering, possibly, why the spikes are there.

DUKE STREET FROM THE CROSS — The Albert Tower dominates the Agricultural Hall in the background (the Agricultural Hall is now better known as the Palace Theatre and Grand Hall). To the left of the furnishing store can be seen a gable blaring the sign "Royal Hotel". Bobby Templeton, possibly Kilmarnock's most famous footballer, and one of Scotland's best in his day, was at one time mine host at the Royal. Christie the cutlers on the left was finally located in Queen Street under the style, A.V. Christie.

LOANHEAD SCHOOL — Loanhead Elementary School opened soon after the start of the present century. The foundation stone was laid by Dunfermline-born Andrew Carnegie, the U.S. steel magnate. Pupils had the option of passing from the primary department to the Advanced Division and leaving at 14, or,if they passed the qualifying examination, continuing their education in the secondary department of Kilmarnock Academy.

DICK INSTITUTE FIRE 1909 — The first floor of the Dick Institute after the fire in 1909 which destroyed most of the museum's collections only eight years after it was opened. With help from organisations like the Glenfield Ramblers and generous benefactors such as Richmond Paton, Sir Alexander Walker and R. McC. Kater, the museum was re-stocked with several good and valuable collections when the Institute was opened again in 1911.

CORNER OF GRANGE STREET AND PARK STREET — The gas-storage tank visible above the trees on the right proves why local people named the slope the 'Gas Brae'. The wall lamp at the corner must have been a boon in the winter to the young woman standing at the top of the stairs.

CO-OPERATIVE FLOUR STORE — The Co-operative flour store which stood in Grange Street on a site now occupied by the D.H.S.S. offices. Flour was stored here, for use in the Co-operative bakehouse in St. Andrews Street.(For the story of the Co-operative Society see Excelsior, The Story of the Co-op.)

DECORATED TRAMCAR, 1911 — Portraits of King George V and Queen Mary flanking a painting of the Imperial Crown suggest Kilmarnock's participation in a Royal event. The tram was, in fact, part of the town's celebration of the coronation in 1911.

PROCLAMATION OF GEORGE V — Crowds thronged the Cross in the summer of 1911 to hear Provost Mathew Smith read the proclamation of the accession of George V to the throne of the United Kingdom. Provost Smith can be seen in the centre of the picture, chain of office round his neck. A platoon of soldiers provides protection on the flanks for the dignitaries. But why the fixed bayonets? Jimmy Shaw presides calmly over the scene, and there, right at the front, is the Burgh Band.

TROOPS ROUTE MARCH, 1911 — This is the Portland Row in Hurlford about the time of the First World War. The soldiers, most of them in their teens, are marching towards Riccarton. The absence of rifles suggests they are not on their way to Hurlford Station to catch the train south. More likely, they are returning from a route march to their encampment at Riccarton (below). If this is the case, then the soldiers on the march are from the 8th Battalion of the Highland Light Infantry. Troops in the 1911 encampment may have taken part in Kilmarnock's celebrations of King George V's coronation. Soldiers marching through the streets was to become an all-too-familiar scene during the 1914-18 war, which cost the lives of 147,609 Scots.

RICCARTON CAMP, 1911

KILMARNOCK BURGH BAND, 1911 — A glance back to the hey-day of the 'burra baun'. This shot of Kilmarnock Burgh Band, 28 musicians in all, was taken in the Howard Park on June, 1911. The huge crowd in the background suggests the Band might have been taking part in local celebrations to mark the Royal Proclamation. Composition of the Band is quite unlike the composition of modern burgh bands. Besides the usual brass, the 1911 Band has a sizeable wood-wind section of flute, clarinet and basoon. There is even a saxophone, an instrument which, strangely, finds little favour in bands and orchestras outside the jazz scene.

SALVATION ARMY — The Riccarton Corps of the Army in 1912. Formed in 1885, the Riccarton Corps complements the work of the Kilmarnock Temple formed three years earlier in 1882. Working from halls in Sturrock Street and Witchknowe Road, the two Corps carry on traditional and extensive work among people over-powered by circumstances beyond their control. The Kilmarnock Temple, broadcasts its evangelistic message with the help of its popular marching band and the songsters.

OLD STREET, RICCARTON — A busy part of the village's extensive shopping area round about 1890 or 1900. Readers could be excused if the thought that "The Cash House" was the proprietor's euphemistic way of describing the local pawn shop. It was, in fact, a baby-linen shop owned by Bobby Todd. In later life, it was to serve as a dry salter's. Watson the baker occupied the shop at the corner.

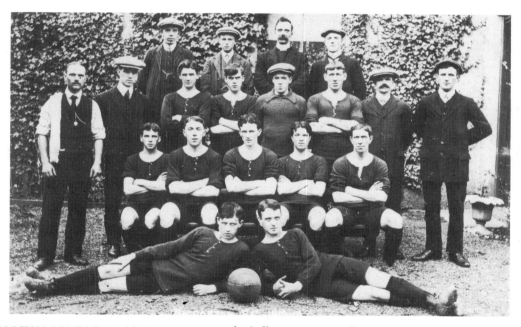

RICCARTON BLUEBELL, 1912 — Riccarton Bluebell Junior Football Team in 1912. Second from the left in the second row is Mr. William McCallum, who was to become a prominent member of the Town Council in the 1950s.

FEVER WAGON, circa 1900 — The fever wagon, as it was called, on its way, possibly, to the Infectious Diseases Hospital (Kilmarnock Infirmary). Date would be about 1900. Seated up front is the doctor, dressed in the manner of his profession in bil't (boiled) shirt and tile hat. Inside the wagon would be the patient. The box behind the doctor and coachman would contain the disinfectants used for 'fumigating' houses hit by fever.

NELSON STREET — A tenement in Nelson Street, clearly in the last stages of disintegration yet still home for many families. The brats (aprons of coarse cloth) worn by the three young women symbolise the drudgery of their lives. Bottom right a man is seen on the Timmer Brig (Timber Bridge) which crosses the Kilmarnock Water to the Sandbed.

THE SANDBED, circa 1900 — Showing a typical tenement with outside staircase. Children play in the cobbles, some poorly dressed, some giving the impression of better circumstances. Before the development of King Street, the Sandbed was Kilmarnock's main thoroughfare. The Laigh Kirk tower and steeple can be seen on the left hand side of the photograph.

PADDY'S BRAE — East George Street, or Paddy's Brae, as the locals called it by dint of the fact that this was the route taken by Irish immigrant labourers from the railway station to the lodging houses. The turreted building in the centre of the picture is one of the two model lodging-houses. On the right is the back entrance to the Transport Station. The tenements and the white-washed cottage have steps leading directly on to the roadway.

DEAN LANE FROM HIGH STREET — The locality where Henry Shields lived. The shop features one of the earliest permanent window advertisements. Adhesive letters spell out one of the nation's favourite chocolates. The children contemplating the jars of sweets may be deciding how to spend their pocket money.

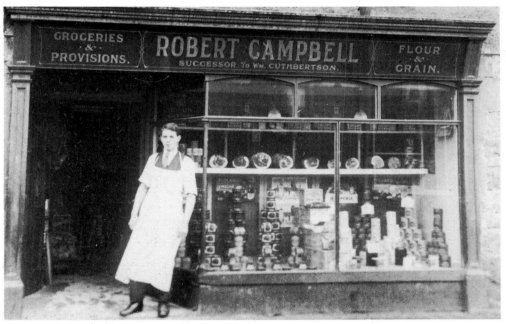

GROCERS SHOP, DEAN LANE — A typical grocers shop, thought to be in Dean Lane, just before the start of the 1914-18 war. Note the uncovered hams, possibly Ayrshire, Belfast and American, smoked and fresh. Note, too, the precarious balance of tins, cans and the giant dummy box of Vulcan matches, common in this kind of window display. An open sack of potatoes lies at the shop entrance.

BLACKWOOD BROS., SPINNING, circa 1917 — Girls tend the flyer twister, a machine which twists two or three strands of wool together at great speed before winding the product on to bobbins. The bobbins are then ready to go to the weaver.

BLACKWOOD BROS., REELING, circa 1917 — This is a reeling machine. The spun wool is wound on to the hexagonal reeler on the left, and removed by the girls in skeins or, as they are called in Scotland, hanks.

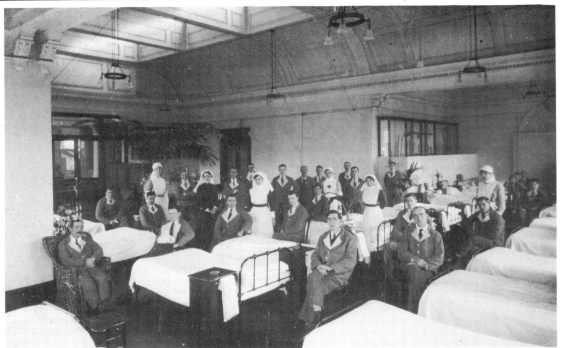

DICK INSTITUTE AS AN AUXILIARY HOSPITAL, 1917 — As casualties mounted on the Western Front, the military authorities requisitioned properties which could be easily adapted to use as hospitals. With 3 spacious rooms on the bottom flat and two equally spacious galleries above, Kilmarnock's Dick Institute library and museum was an obvious choice. In 1917, the Institute became an Auxiliary Hospital. Above we see matron and nurses and patients posing for photographs in Ward 5 located in one of the upper galleries. Below: Soldiers enjoy the therapy of billiards, carpet bowling and the gramophone in the games room (Art Gallery).

THE KITCHEN — Nurses performing the duties of cook in the Dick Institute Kitchen.

THE PEACE TREE, 1920 — The scene in the Howard Park in 1920 at the planting of a tree in thanksgiving for the end of the Great War of 1914-18. The peace tree stands between the park lodge and the cabin.

GOOD OLD KILLIE, 1920 — Riccarton supporters of Kilmarnock Football Club about to set out on the journey to Hampden Park, to see their team play Albion Rovers in the final of the Scottish (Victory) Cup in 1920. The journey, in John Craig's lorry couldn't have been comfortable, but not one of the fans would notice that especially on the way back. Kilmarnock beat Albion 3-2 and were following their fans back to town with the Cup.

SCOTTISH CUP WINNERS, 1920 — A record crowd of 95,000, paying a record sum of £3,396, turned up at Hampden Park to see Kilmarnock and Albion Rovers contest the Scottish (Victory) Cup Final of 1920. Albion scored in the 5th minute but, by half-time, a goal by Willie Culley had tied the score at 1-1. Mattha Shortt gave Kilmarnock a 2-1 lead in the second-half, and, though Albion fought back to 2-2, Kilmarnock finished winners thanks to a third goal by J.R. Smith.

Team, Third Row:— T. Hamilton, T. Blair, D. Gibson. Second Row:— J. McNaught, M. Smith, J.R. Smith, W. Culley, M. McPhail. Front Row:— A. Mackie, M. Shortt, R. Neave, J. Bagan.

TRAVELLING PEOPLE — Judging from their dress, these travelling people were taking a day off from metal work, basketry and door-to-door selling. Gypsies frequently camped in the environs of Kilmarnock. One of the most popular encampments **was** a clearing near the Reid Bridge at Struthers Steps. They were there most of the summer and with their clothes pins, beautifully made baskets and talent for patching metal pails, were welcome at many a door.

TURNER & EWING ALBION, 1921 — Founded in 1810, Turner and Ewing had a high reputation for the quality of their bottled mineral waters. This is one of their Albion lorries used to deliver their products to shops, restaurants, cafes and private houses. The money bag worn by the driver was a typical accessory of those who followed the same kind of occupation. In addition to Turner and Ewing, the town could boast two other manufacturers of mineral waters, Rankin and Borland and Caldwell.

WATERLOO STREET c. 1920 — The handcart on the right is parked near Star Inn Close, home of the printing shop where John Wilson published the First Edition of the Works of Robert Burns in 1786. The Bridge bears the inscription 'Flood, 14th July, 1852'. During this flood, the Flesh Market Bridge acted more like a dam than a water channel. The water level rose so sharply that, within minutes, the Cross was under deep and deepening water, (see Water, Water, Everywhere).

FORE STREET — One of the oldest parts of Kilmarnock leading to the town centre and one of the first slum areas to be cleared, but not before the 1920s. This picture has been taken looking towards the railway bridge.

BANK PLACE — A salubrious extension of Kilmarnock as it broke free of the over-crowded town centre. It was an area which immediately attracted the professional classes. Serving as a back-drop to the scene is the building which was to become the Bank of Scotland as it is today.

THE BANK OF SCOTLAND — Founded in 1695, the Bank of Scotland, unlike the Bank of England had no role as an agent of government. The Bank was forbidden to lend money to the state and had to rely on Scotland's agriculture, industry and commerce for its business survival. The Kilmarnock branch which stood in Low Church Lane was one of the first branches opened in Scotland.

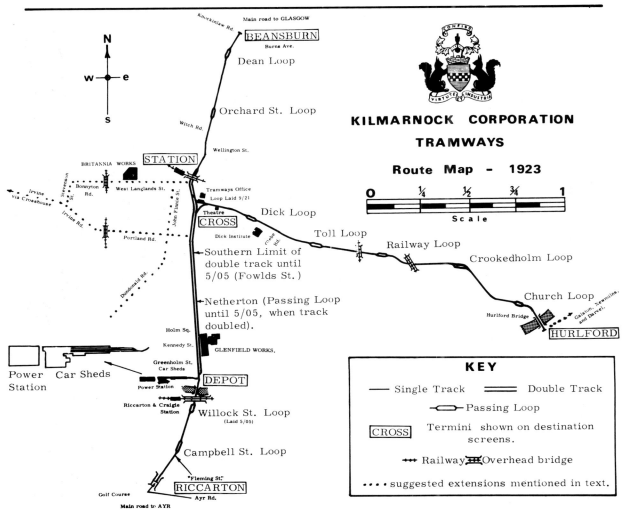

KILMARNOCK CORPORATION TRAMWAYS

TRAMWAYS

Route Map – 1923

Scale

KEY

— Single Track   ══ Double Track

⬭ Passing Loop

CROSS   Termini shown on destination screens.

⟷ Railway   ⚏ Overhead bridge

•••• suggested extensions mentioned in text.

KILMARNOCK CORPORATION TRAMWAYS.

FARES AND STAGES.

Minimum Fare for Passengers of 14 years and over, 1d.

BEANSBURN & RICCARTON SECTION.

STAGE.	FARE.
Ayr Road Boundary to Fleming Street - -	1d
Fleming Street to Netherton Street - -	1d
Netherton Street to the Cross - -	1d
Cross to Orchard Street - -	1d
Orchard Street to Beansburn - -	1d
Ayr Road Boundary and Netherton Street -	1½d
Fleming Street and Railway Station -	1½d
Netherton Street and Orchard Street -	1½d
Cross and Beansburn - -	1½d
Ayr Road Boundary and Railway Station -	2d
Fleming Street and Orchard Street - -	2d
Netherton Street and Beansburn - -	2d
Ayr Road Boundary and Beansburn - -	3d

(Minimum Fare, 1d.)

Fares for Labouring Classes.

	JOURNEYS.		
	2	4	6
Ayr Road Boundary and Railway Station -	2d	4d	6d
Kennedy Street and Orchard Street -	2d	4d	6d
St. Marnock Street and Beansburn -	2d	4d	6d
Double Through Fare - -	4d	8d	—

(Minimum Fare, 2d.)

HURLFORD SECTION.

STAGE.	FARE
Railway Station to Glebe Road or Melville Street -	1d
Glebe Road to Railway Loop - - -	1d
Railway Loop to Crookedholm - - -	1d
Crookedholm to Hurlford - - -	1d
Railway Station and London Road Toll - -	1½d
Glebe Road and Crookedholm - - -	1½d
London Road Toll and Hurlford - - -	1½d
Railway Station and Crookedholm - -	2d
Glebe Road and Hurlford - - -	2d
Through Fare - - -	3d

(Minimum Fare, 1d.)

Fares for Labouring Classes.

	JOURNEYS.		
	2	4	6
Railway Station and Railway Loop -	2d	4d	6d
Glebe Road and Crookedholm -	2d	4d	6d
London Road Toll and Hurlford -	2d	4d	6d
Through Fare -	4d	8d	—

(Minimum Fare, 2d.)

Children under three years of age Free; over three, and under fourteen, Half the Ordinary Fare; ½ being the Minimum Charge.
Only bona-fide Workers of these Classes can obtain two-journey, four-journey, and six-journey tickets from all Conductors of Workmen and Regular Service Cars up till 8 a.m. These tickets are not available after 6.30 on week days, and 2 p.m. on Saturdays. Overtime Permits from Employers are now cancelled.
The Public are requested to report in writing to the Tramway Manager any want of civility on the part of any Tramway Servant, also any irregularity which they may witness. For tracing purposes it is only necessary to give the alphabetical letters and number of their Ticket, or the Time with Police number or Route number of Car.

HURLFORD CROSS — Hurlford Cross as it was just before the start of the tramcar service to Kilmarnock in 1904.

FIRST OPEN TOP TRAMCAR — Kilmarnock's first open top tramcar appeared on the streets of the town in July, 1905. It came straight from London where it had been put on show by the makers at an electric tramway and railway exhibition, hence its popular description 'the exhibition car'.

SANDY MACKIE — Two pipers lead a procession from the Cross into Cheapside Street past Rankin and Borland, the chemists. The piper on the right is thought to be Sandy Mackie, famous in the annals of Kilmarnock for a journey which he made from Kilmarnock to Edinburgh backwards and harnessed to a pram.

THE EMPIRE — The Empire Picture-house in Titchfield Street opened in 1913. The Empire enjoyed a great popularity with Kilmarnock's picture-goers for over 50 years. It was the only building of its kind in town with a side balcony, which allowed patrons to enjoy a 'dress circle' view at a little less than the top price. A fire brought the Empire to the end of its days in 1965.

KILMARNOCK CORPORATION MOTOR BUS — One of the four Kilmarnock Corporation motor buses which took over the Hurlford run when the tram-cars were taken out of service on 15th December, 1926. This bus was an Albion, made by the Albion Motor Company Ltd., of Glasgow. These along with eight Thorneycrofts gave the Council a fleet of 12 motor buses to take over entirely from the tram-cars. The buses proved faster and more economical than the trams, so much so that, on 31st December, 1931, the Council sold their Corporation Motor Bus undertaking to Sir William Thomson's S.M.T, later to become Western S.M.T.

KILMARNOCK HARRIER AND ATHLETIC CLUB, 1924 — From its inception in 1887, the Club has had an outstanding record at local and national level in track and cross-country events. As early as 1889, when the Club was only two years old, J. McWilliams won the Scottish harriers-union championship. Between 1978 and 1987, Gregor Grant won nine consecutive Ayrshire senior cross-country championships, a feat not likely to be emulated. The current year (1989) has seen Club members win a host of Scottish championships from junior right through senior to veteran level. At the British level, they can boast Hugh Rankin (British 3,000 metres indoor champion over 50s) and have had two representatives in British squads, Mary McClung and Alan Murray. The club, which now has in excess of 150 members, trains at Scott-Ellis Playingfield and operates under the title, Johnnie Walker (Kilmarnock) Harrier and Athletic Club.

SAXONE, MAKING DEPARTMENT 1928 — Tradesmen and apprentices of the Saxone Shoe Company's Kilmarnock factory in 1928. Origin of the Saxone goes back to 1820 and the formation of Messrs. Clark and Son, a firm principally engaged in hand shoe making for the Brazilian market. In 1873, the firm, now styled A.L. Clark and Company, opened a steam-powered boot and shoe factory in Titchfield Street. Thirty five years later, in 1908, the firm assumed yet another style, Saxone Shoe Company Ltd., and it was under the trade name Saxone, that it became famous the world over for the high quality of its footwear. Taken over by the British Shoe Corporation, the Saxone was closed in the 1960's.

SAXONE FACTORY c. 1930 — The Saxone factory on the banks of Kilmarnock Water, as it was before demolition, along with Titchfield Street property, to make way for the Galleon Leisure Centre.

THE FLITTING OF JIMMY SHAW, 1929 — Under the supervision of Mr. Thomas McDowall, stonemason, the statue of Jimmy Shaw was transferred from the Cross, where he had stood since 1848, and moved to his present site near the Dick Institute.

KILMARNOCK'S DICK WHITTINGTON — Son of a Riccarton farmer, James Shaw was born in 1764. After a rudimentary education at Grammar School, Kilmarnock, he spent a few years working in the United States, but returned to Britain at the age of 20 and took the road to London. James Shaw, or Jimmy Shaw, as he was popularly called, rose high and quickly in London society. In 1805, he was elected Lord Mayor of London and, the following year, he led the public procession at the funeral of Lord Nelson. Shaw's services to London brought him a baronetcy in 1809. The distinction which Jimmy Shaw earned himself in London, his patronage of the arts, and his generosity to Kilmarnock persuaded the Town Council to raise a statue in his memory. About £1,000 was collected and Mr. James Fillans, using a portrait by Tannock, (one of Shaw's **proteges**) fashioned the statue from Carrara marble.

SCHOOLS CUP CHAMPIONS, 1929 — When this photograph was taken, the annual schools football competition run by Kilmarnock and District Schools attracted very big crowds. This is a photograph of the Grammar (Kilmarnock) School team which won the Kilmarnock and District Schools Cup in 1929. The Schools Cup final was played at Rugby Park before a crowd of many thousands.

Included in this picture are: Robert Toole (teacher), David McCulloch, John Christie, John McIntosh (teacher), George Brown (head master), Alec Morrison (teacher), David Robertson, David Richardson (captain), Willie Wood.

SCOTTISH CUP WINNERS, 1928-29 — The Kilmarnock Football Club team which gave Kilmarnock the Scottish Cup for the second time by defeating Rangers 2-0 at Hampden in the final of 1929. Inspired goalkeeping by Sam Clemie and second-half goals by Daddler Aitken and Jimmy Williamson brought victory to Rugby Park.

TEAM MEMBERS: Back Row, L to R: T. Robertson, S. Clemie, J. Nibloe. Middle Row: W. Connell, H. Cunningham, J. Weir, M. Smith, J. Ramsay, J. Williamson, J. Aitken, Front Row: H. Morton, H. McLaren, J. Dunlop, J. McEwan.

ACADEMY STREET — Academy Street, Riccarton, awash in the 1932 floods. More than 150 families were rescued in horse-drawn carts. The Power Station, Glenfield, Barr Thomsons and many other factories were flooded (see Water, Water Everywhere).

CAMPBELL STREET BRIDGE — The Campbell Street bridge at Riccarton during the 1932 flood. Heavy rain from Hogmanay to the 3rd of January caused both the Kilmarnock and Irvine rivers to overflow, resulting in serious flooding of the lower areas of Kilmarnock.

KING STREET IN THE 1930s — **A Riley** sports car passes Dr. Robertson's surgery at the junction with Fowlds Street. The shops huddled at the foot of King Street Church include Carrick the butcher, Boyle the drysalter and Paterson the grocer.

THE EVENT THAT NEVER WAS — When King George V died in 1936, his eldest son, Edward, Prince of Wales, was proclaimed King as Edward VIII. 1937 was declared the year for the coronation of Edward VIII. The whole country prepared for the event and Kilmarnock was no exception. Banners, bunting and flags were taken down sooner than expected as King Edward **abdicated** in order to marry American divorcee, Mrs Simpson. Edward's younger brother, George, was later crowned King George VI.

TRANSPORT STATION, c. 1930 — The Western SMT bus station, or transport station as it was more popularly called, in Portland Street. An inspector plays policeman in the middle of the road to see that the double-decker can emerge safely and turn south towards the Cross.

DUKE STREET — Duke Street in the 1920s, with hand–carts out numbering motor cars. The post box outside Duke Street Town Sub-Office can be seen on the pavement on the right. Beyond the car on the left there is a glimpse of the elegant Victorian canopy which shielded the goods displayed in the last two or three shops before Green Street.

THE FIRST TROPHY – The Kilmarnock Cricket Club team which won the Rowan Charity Cup in 1936, the first trophy to be won by the Club.
Standing L to R: H. Fulton, J.L. Speirs, E.J. MacKenzie, J. Climie, A. Johnston, J. Lindsay (scorer), Seated: R.J. Ritchie, A. Miller, T. Ferguson (captain), G. Hill, J.R. McDougall. In Front: T. Bell, G. Millar.

JIM AITCHISON

AITCHISON IN ACTION AT LORDS

"Arguably the best batsman Scotland has ever produced". This was the tribute paid to Jim Aitchison by clubmate Nisbet Gallagher, wrting in *The Golden Years, 1952-1976*. During a playing career for Kilmarnock stretching from 1937 to 1967, Aitchison scored a Scottish record total of 31,051 runs at an average of 45.7. He hit 61 centuries and 230 fifties. Aitchison's dominance of Scottish cricket was powerfully demonstrated in his international career. Between 1946 and 1963, he played for Scotland on 69 occasions, amassed 3,669 runs, including seven centuries and 25 fifties. Highlights included 100 against **Australia** at Hamilton Crescent in 1956, 106 not **out** against South Africa in 1947, and, what was then a Scottish record, 190 not out against Ireland in 1959.

ROYAL INSPECTION — The scene when King George VI reviewed Kilmarnock Civil Defence Services in Howard Park in June 1942.

DAD'S ARMY, 1943 — Kilmarnock greets 'Dad's Army.' The Provost takes the salute as the Irvine Company of the Home Guard marches past the Town Hall in May, 1943.

MAYOR WALTER HARVEY — The two men on the **left** are natives of Kilmarnock and live in Kilmarnock — 3,000 miles apart from each other. Mayor Walter Harvey of Kilmarnock, Virginia (left), has come to Kilmarnock (the original) to **convey** greetings from his fellow townspeople. The Mayor's visit was made to return an earlier visit which Provost Daniel Cairns of Auld Killie made to Mayor Harvey and Kilmarnock, Virginia. Our photograph shows Mayor Harvey and Provost Cairns exchanging gifts and greetings in the Town Hall in July 1949, while Town Clerk, Mr. W.L. Walker looks on.

KILMARNOCK SPECIALS — The 5th Division of Kilmarnock Special Constables, 1944. The 'Specials' assisted the official police force in their wartime duties and were disbanded shortly after the war.

KILMARNOCK TECHNICAL COLLEGE IN THE 1930s — Long an adjunct of Kilmarnock Academy, the College was opened just after the start of the century. The College took the place of the existing Science and Art School, and, in filling this role, relieved the new Kilmarnock Academy of giving over space for the establishment of chemical and physical laboratories.

KILMARNOCK CRICKET CLUB, 1946 — The Kilmarnock Cricket Team which, in 1946, won the Western District Union Championship for the first time.
Back Row: T.A.B. Shedden, T. Bell, G. Millar, G. Hill. Middle Row: J. Murray (scorer), M. Colquhoun, G. Wilson (professional), R.D. Walker, C.L. Ancell, J.L. Muir, J. Aitchison, J. Sinclair (Match Secretary). Front Row: H. Fulton, J. Rome (President), R.J. Ritchie (Captain), C.F. Douglas (Vice-President), A.S. McCulloch.

DICK INSTITUTE LENDING LIBRARY — The lending library as it was in 1948. Mr. David Lawrence, the librarian, chats to a member of staff at the reception counter.

DICK INSTITUTE READING ROOM — Lecterns in the reading room held the most popular daily newspapers, with others available on the tables. This room now contains the reference and audio library.

KILMARNOCK AMATEURS, 1956 — League champions and winners of the League Cup, Kilmarnock amateurs, nursery team to Kilmarnock's 1st Division team, scored 257 goals in 45 games in 1956.

MARGARET McDOWALL — Margaret McDowall dominated British women's back-stroke swimming in the 1950s. At the age of 14, Margaret was a member of the first Scottish team to win the Bologna Trophy. In 1951, she equalled the 100-yards British native record, and won both the senior and junior championships. In 1952, Margaret reached the final of the 100-yards at the Helsinki Olympics, and followed this by becoming the first woman to win the British 100-yards championship in three successive years. At the 1954 Vancouver Commonwealth Games, Margaret was a member of the British team which broke the 300 yards medley record. In 1958, she won the Scottish senior 100 yards championship for the eighth year running.

MASSEY-HARRIS, 1951 — Taking part in the "Festival of Britain" parade is a Massey-Harris tractor, probably made in Coventry or Manchester, drawing a Massey-Harris baler, made in Kilmarnock. Massey-Harris, later to become Massey-Ferguson, started up in Moorfield Industrial Estate in 1948 and provided work for many thousands of men and women for some 30 years. The tractor is passing Dr. Robertson's house and surgery/dispensary at the junction of King Street and Fowlds Street. Beyond that, in the direction of the Cross, there was a group of popular commercial premises — Rodger the newsagent, McLauchlan the fruiterer, Campbell the wireless, bicycle and pram dealer and the King's Bar.

KILMARNOCK PIPE BAND — Seen here in full Highland dress marching along St. Andrew's Street, watched appreciatively by local tenement residents. And just look at that road surface. Not a pot-hole or carriage crossing in sight. The tower of King Street Church looks down upon the scene.

SANDBED BRIDGE IN THE 1950's — The "Old Bridge" or "Town's Bridge", as it was also known, is the oldest of Kilmarnock's bridges. Earliest mention of the bridge was made by Timothy Pont who visited Kilmarnock in the early years of the 17th century. "A faire stone bridge over the river Marnock" was how he described it. The lade was used originally to power a waukmill and a cornmill near the Cross. Women in the waukmill beat woollen cloth which had been soaked, in order to shrink and clean the fabric.

THE PRE-FABS — First of the factory-built houses to appear in Kilmarnock in the early years following the 1939/45 war. These houses in Altonhill Avenue, and others of their kind in other parts of the town, were called 'temporaries' by dint of the fact that they were meant to last no more than 20 years. Though the 'temporaries' have all disappeared now, their life was prolonged beyond its allotted span by cladding them in bricks.

CORNER OF FOWLDS STREEET AND QUEEN STREET — This tenement property was demolished to make way for the road which filters north/south traffic to the east of the town's main shopping and commercial area. The corner shop belonged to Miss Annie MacDonald and sold groceries, confectionery and newspapers. In the left foreground is one of the first Vauxhalls, probably built in the late **1940s**. In front of this a Vauxhall Cresta, a popular model in the **50s** and **60s**.

A TYPICAL BACKYARD IN QUEEN STREET, **1950s** — Many houses in Queen Street and Clark Street were hovels and in no way suitable for family life. Their demolition helped to clear the way for the internal by-pass and advance the Council's post-war, slum clearance programme.

CORNER OF ROBERTSON PLACE AND GILMOUR STREET — Besides owning the fruit shop, Fred Burley sold fruit and vegetables from a horse-drawn lorry. Next door was Angelo Mocogni's Newton Ice Cream Saloon. Angie's saloon was one of the first in Kilmarnock to install a one-arm bandit. Sitting accommodation and an excellent product made 'Angie's' a popular meeting place. The garret window, in the roof was a common feature of the architecture of Robertson Place.

THE BRIDGE INN, ROBERTSON PLACE — Taken in the 1950s, this picture shows the end of Robertson Place furthest from the Cross. Opposite the Bridge Inn stood the rival Bellfield Tavern. Next to the Inn Mrs Stewart's wee shop was one of many 'open all hours'. Mrs Stewart sold life's essentials, ranging from bread and butter to candles and matches, not forgetting sweets.

PROCLAMATION OF SUCCESSION OF QUEEN ELIZABETH II — Scene at the Cross in 1952, as the town Clerk, Mr. James Nicol, is reading the Proclamation of Queen Elizabeth in succession to her father, King George VI.

Those assembled here include: Baillie Maisie Garven, Bailie Robert Banks, Provost Alexander Clark, Bailie William Gilmour, Bailie Kennedy, Mr. James Scott and councillors Wilcox, McCallum, Rome, Cairns, Cunningham, Abbott and Beattie.

THE KIRKIN' O' THE COUNCIL — The traditional ceremony of the Kirkin' o' the Council, taken from a photograph in Kilmarnock Standard Annual 1955.

BELLFIELD HOUSE, 1955 — Gifted to the people of Kilmarnock and Riccarton Parishes in 1875 by the three daughters of Mr. George Buchanan, Bellfield **featured** the mansionhouse, a rock garden with pond, a walled garden, a conservatory and a play area. In accordance with the **Buchanans'** wishes the parishioners were free to make full recreational use of the estate. With its superb amenities, Bellfield was a popular picnic area.

BELLFIELD HOUSE AND ROCK GARDENS — The increasing cost of repairs and maintenance persuaded trustees to feu some of the land of Bellfield to Kilmarnock **Town Council** for houses. Over 1800 were built. Tragically, Bellfield House has been demolished, the rock garden and walled garden are gone. Happily however, Bellfield is still fulfilling the **Buchanans'** wishes, as a place for public enjoyment, with a play area for children, tennis courts, football pitches and a bowling green.

MOUNT HOUSE — Opening of Kilmarnock's second home for old people, The Mount, in the 1950s. Councillor Tom Ryan, convener of the Council's Health Committee, is in the centre.

INTERNATIONAL BURNS FESTIVAL — A meeting of east and west which would have pleased Robert Burns. In 1955, Kilmarnock hosted the Burns International Festival, a kind of rehearsal of what was planned for celebration of the 200th **anniversary** of the poet's birth in 1959. Delegates from Australia, Canada, Rhodesia, USSR and India attended. Here we see the Russian delegate, Dr. Elistratova **and** Provost William Gilmour laying memorial wreaths at the foot of the Poet's statue in Kay Park.

SCOTTISH RINK CHAMPIONS — The West Netherton bowlers who won the Scottish Rink Championship at Queens Park in 1956. (Photograph taken by Stuart McLauchlan from one in the Kilmarnock Standard Annual).

AYRSHIRE BOWLERS — Won all three titles, singles, pairs and rink, in the 1957 S.B.A. championships at Glasgow. Singles champion, W.D. Jones (Ardrossan), is in the centre of the front row with rink champions R. Findlay, R. McKinlay, A. Halliday and S. Stewart, skip (Ayr Craigie), on his left and pairs champions, John D. Pollock and Robert B. M'Call (Kilmarnock), on his right. Behind Mr. Pollock is Mr. N.D. Robinson (Springhill), president of the Scottish Bowling Association.

MASS-RADIOGRAPHY CAMPAIGN — The first national mass-radiography campaign against tuberculosis was mounted by the National Health Service in 1957. Kilmarnock gave the campaign full support. This reproduction of a photograph in the Kilmarnock Standard Annual shows Mr. Gavin Ralston, then senior surgeon at Kilmarnock Infirmary, who was among the first to be x-rayed in the mobile unit stationed outside the Palace Theatre.

GRAND HALL DANCING — In an attempt to provide entertainment for the town's young people in the post-war years, the Town Council sponsored public dancing in the Grand Hall. The sessions enjoyed a long period of popularity with dancers and spectators. The well-oiled, 'short back 'n' sides' hairstyles of the youngsters gives this shot a distinct flavour of the 1950s. Still later, the Grand Hall was used for roller skating.

A BARCLAY SPECIAL — This Barclay steam locomotive looks like some others of its class. But there is something about the loco which makes it unique, and demonstrates the engineering versatility of Barclay's. Instead of burning coal, this loco burns palm kernels in a specially-designed firebox. Built in 1962, it is still working in Indonesia.

STREET WELL — A gravitation street well which made its appearance in the second half of last century. Wells like this were still in use far into the present century.

KILMARNOCK STANDARD CENTENARY ISSUE, 1963 — The Kilmarnock Standard began its career in 1863, a Liberal rival to the Conservative Kilmarnock Herald. The picture on the left shows Peter Murray, one of the compositors, setting type for the centenary edition, printed in June 1963.

WILLIE McALLISTER, FOREMAN PRINTER — Willie makes the vital examination of the first copy of the week's issue of Kilmarnock Standard. If the print is bold and clear with no mistakes, a nod from Willie sets the old Goss press churning out its 25,000 copies. In those days, the Standard was a broadsheet locally owned. Today, the Standard is a tabloid, owned by Scottish and Universal Newspapers.

DANIEL CAIRNS — Watched by Provost Daniel Cunningham and the Town Clerk, Mr W.L. Walker, Councillor Daniel Cairns signs the Roll which made him a Burgess, or Freeman, of Kilmarnock in November, 1964. Probably Kilmarnock's most prominent Councillor this century, Mr. Cairns had given 33 years continuous service to the Council when he received the honour. During this period, he had served **twice as Provost from 1946 to 1950 and from 1956 to 1959.** The Burgess Ticket notes Councillor Cairns's "distinguished service to local government" and "the high respect and esteem in which he was held by the community."

QUEEN'S VISIT, 1962 — A memorable day in July 1962. Councillor Daniel Cairns, senior magistrate, accompanies H.M. Queen Elizabeth to her car in Elmbank Drive at the conclusion of a 25-minute visit to Kilmarnock in the course of a tour of Ayrshire.

(Our photograph is a copy of one by Stuart McLauchlan which appeared in the Kilmarnock Standard Annual).

LEAGUE CHAMPIONS, 1965 — Season 1964/65 was a memorable one for Kilmarnock Football Club. Runners-up (the previous season), in the First Division (the 1965 equivalent of today's Premier League) Kilmarnock came to the last game of the season still with a chance of winning the championship. Only Hearts could deny them the honour. Dramatically the fates had decided that both contenders would meet in the decider at Tynecastle. Hearts stood top of the table with 50 points and a goal average of 1.91: Kilmarnock were second with 48 points and an average of 1.86. For Hearts, a draw would give them the championship. Kilmarnock had to win by at least two goals. The day and the Championship went to Kilmarnock. Davie Sneddon and Brian McIlroy scored the goals which gave them a 2-0 victory — and a goal-average just .04 above the Hearts average (see You'll Never Walk Alone).

Back Row L to R: T. McLean, R. Black, R. Ferguson, D. Sneddon, B. McIlroy. Middle Row: W. Waddell (Manager), E. Murray, J. McGrory, J. McInally, F. Beattie (Captain), M. Watson, A. King, W. McCrae (Trainer). Front Row: T. Lauchlan (Director), R.B. Thyne (Director), W. McIvor (Chairman), D.R. McCulloch (Director), T. Kerr (Director).

TRIPLE WINNERS —
The Kilmarnock Cricket Club team which, in 1965, won the Rowan Cup, the West League Cup and the Ayrshire Cup.

Standing : G.M. Love, A. Trangmer, J. Lennie, R. Ellis, H. Ferguson, J.M. Clark. Seated: J. Aitchison, T.N. Gallacher, R.G. Hill (Captain), A. Johnston, J. Thomson.

SPRINGHILL — Springhill Eventide Home which provides in-house care for elderly residents. The sheltered houses in the foreground, built in 1966, are home to those who are able to live on their own, watched over by the staff of the 'big House'.

TOWNHOLM RENTS REBELLION — Tenants of council houses in Townholm gather outside the Council Chamber to protest against Council plans to impose equal rents for equal accommodation. Townholm housing being much inferior to the general standard of other council housing, the tenants protest persuaded the Council to give up their plans. (See The Tragedy of Townholm).

KILMARNOCK CROSS, 1964 — From the 1950s, an ever-increasing number of motor cars in the area led to traffic-flow problems for Kilmarnock. The round-about in the centre of the Cross was one attempt to resolve these problems. In 1966, a north/south one-way system was introduced.

TRAFFIC JAM, 1964 — The queue of traffic extends along Duke Street, past the Grand Hall and for who knows how far along the London Road. The easing of traffic congestion was one of the reasons for redevelopment of the town centre in the 1970s. John Menzies shop stands on the corner of Regent Street and Duke Street, two of the streets which were to disappear in the 70s.

KILMARNOCK CROSS, c. 1960 — Kilmarnock Cross with its 'buttonhole' round-about as viewed from Duke Street. The elegant blend of the buildings leading from King Street to Portland Street bears testimony to the skill of the architects. The buildings are designed, not only to be functional, but to blend with their surroundings.

DEMOLITION OF KING STREET CHURCH — Scaffolding cocoons King Street Church as workmen demolish it in 1966. Built in 1832, the church had a spire which reached 120 feet into the sky. Its bell, the largest in the town, could be heard all over Kilmarnock and, in favourable circumstances, in neighbouring villages. The 4-dial clock could be seen in most districts of the town. The ground on which the Church stood is now occupied by a shopping development.

COUNCIL HOUSING — Cottages and flats in Wilson Avenue, Middleton Park, where Kilmarnock's first Corporation houses were built just after the end of the 1914-18 war.

THE CHEENY BUILDINGS — The well-known china (cheeny) tenements in North Hamilton Street in the 1960s. The glazed white bricks were possibly made in the local Southhook Pottery.

ONTHANK HOUSING — Two-storey flats in Arness Terrace, part of the 1500-house Onthank estate which grew up in the 1960s.

BELLFIELD — This attractive suite of shops and flats in Whatriggs Road was built by the Town Council in the new housing estate of Bellfield. It was a demonstration of Council policy to do what they could to give communities on the outskirts of the town as many town-centre amenities as possible.

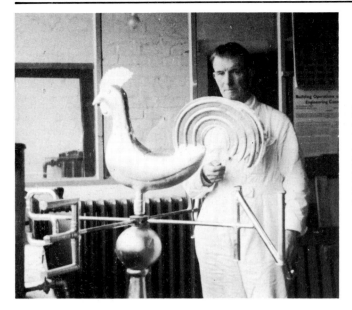

LAIGH KIRK WEATHER COCK — The weather cock was repaired and restored in 1968 after being damaged in a storm. The work was undertaken by the Corporation Direct Labour Department under Mr. Alex Marshall. Mr. John Knox, who applied the finishing touches, is seen here admiring the work.

THE ANTEEKS — Pictured here at the Burns Monument, 'The Anteeks' were one of Kilmarnock's more successful bands in the 1960s. They were a six-man band; consisting of Frank Knapp (singer), George Butler (drums), Jim Condron (bass guitar), Malcolm McNally (keyboards), Billy Gray (guitar), and Jimmy Thomson who was nicknamed 'Hilltone' after a product he used to dye his hair. The Anteeks went to London and, although they were quickly signed up and made their first record, chart success evaded them.

FREEDOM OF THE BURGH — One of Kilmarnock Town Council's last acts as a local authority before handing new power to the new Kilmarnock and Loudoun District Council and Strathclyde Regional Council in 1975 was to confer the freedom of the burgh on three men who had given outstanding service to the local community. Here we see Provost Mrs Maisie Garven with the new Freemen — Lord Howard de Walden, Canon Matthew Littleton and Mr. William Ross. Lord Howard de Walden, whose father restored Dean Castle (damaged by fire in 1735) gifted the Castle and its contents of medieaval armour, musical instruments and tapestries, to the town. Canon Littleton, a native of County Clare, took over as priest at St. Jospeh's, Kilmarnock, in 1952. A member of the Chapter of Canons, he served on the local area Sub-education Committee and on the Crime Prevention Panel. Mr. Ross was elected Labour M.P. for Kilmarnock in 1946. From 1964 to 1970 he served as Secretary of State for Scotland. He was re-appointed to the office under a Labour government in 1974 and retired from politics as Lord Ross of Marnock.

DEMOLITION OF THE COOLING TOWERS — Kilmarnock Power Station, which began generating electricity in 1904, ended its life dramatically with the demolition of its two 190-feet cooling towers in June 1976. The camera catches the moment when the first tower buckles and cracks under the explosive force of 40 lbs. of TNT. The second tower lasted only a few minutes longer.

TITCHFIELD STREET AND SURROUNDING AREA IN THE 1960s — In this photograph we have indicated some of the landmarks which no longer exist or have been considerably changed due to redevelopment: 1. Armour Street, 2. Kilmarnock Swimming Baths, 3. St. Andrew's Street, 4. Princes Street, 5. Plaza Picture House, 6. King Street Church, 7. Saxone Shoe Factory.

KILMARNOCK TOWN CENTRE BEFORE REDEVELOPMENT IN THE 1970s — In this photograph we have indicated some of the landmarks which no longer exist or have been considerably changed due to redevelopment: 1. Duke Street, 2. Dick Brothers Garage, 3. Car Park bounded by Fore Street and Regent Street, 4. Waterloo Street, 5. Town Hall, 6. Plaza Picture House, 7. Burgh Police Station.

DUKE STREET — The corner of Duke Street and Green Street before redevelopment (1972). To the left of the Salon is Crook's the chemist. The upper floors were used as a hotel with entrance in Duke Street between the Salon and the chemist's.

KILMARNOCK BURGH POLICE HEADQUARTERS — Graphic evidence why Kilmarnock town centre was re-constructed in the 1970s. Here we are looking down on a major part of the area which has been re-developed. The Police Office on the left looks in the poorest of health, while to the right of centre, Waterloo Street seems in danger of being engulfed in its own buildings as it squeezes its way into the Cross.

KILMARNOCK CROSS, c. 1970 — Absence of the bell tower of Kilmarnock's old Townhouse which stood at the north end of King Street dates this view of the Corss at around 1970. Though demolition of the townhouse has been effected, the Cross still retians its character as the hub of a busy, thriving town.

THE TOWN BELL — The bell is seen here after having been retrieved from the tower of the old Town Hall, when demolished in 1970. The bell is now in the Civic Centre awaiting the time when it can be put on view.

WESTERN S.M.T. BUS STATION — Pictured here in 1972, the bus station was demolished shortly afterwards in the preparation stages of Kilmarnock's redevelopment.

THE START OF REDEVELOPMENT — The Cross, King Street, Portland Street and Fore Street in the early 1970s before redevelopment of the town centre.

TOWN CENTRE DEVELOPMENT — Bottom left, steel rods are in position, ready to reinforce columns which will take the weight of a concrete bridge over the Kilmarnock Water, on top of which shops now stand. The concrete pillars standing here form the main supports for Woolworths, the Kilmarnock Centre and Burns Shopping Mall.

CONSTRUCTION — It is hard to believe that the foundations pictured here were to turn into the Kilmarnock Centre and bus station. The multi-storey car park is at a more advanced state of development. The old timber signal box, in the background, was one of the first of its kind and controlled rail traffic through Kilmarnock station.

GLENFIELD — Following the example of much of British industry since the late 1970s, the Glenfield had to slim down. The offices in Low Glencairn Street (above) were demolished in 1982, together with part of the works. In the picture below, we see a car emerging from the Glencairn Industrial Estate which now occupies the site of the Glenfield and Kennedy buildings. The world-famous Glenfield water-control equipment is now produced in Kilmarnock by Biwater Valves Ltd., (see From Acorn to Oak).

McLELLAND DRIVE — With an ever-growing demand for housing from an ever-increasing population, the sandstone flats of McLelland Drive were built around the start of the century. The red sandstone flats were built of stone from Ballochmyle Quarry.

RENNIE STREET — Another example of the sturdy private houses built around the start of the century with Ballochmyle sandstone.

WOODSTOCK SCHOOL — One of the latest of Kilmarnock's 13 primary schools. Woodstock School occupies a site at the corner of North Hamilton Street and Woodstock Street. The site was occupied originally by one of Kilmarnock's first Academies. Built in 1875, Tudor Elizabethan in style, the Academy was re-named Hamilton School when the present Kilmarnock Academy was opened in the early 1900s.

GRANGE ACADEMY — Quadrangle of Grange Academy opened in 1967. A town with a population of around 48,000, Kilmarnock has four Academies; Kilmarnock Academy (the oldest), St. Jospeh's Academy, Grange and James Hamilton Academy. Previously located off the London Road, James Hamilton Academy moved to its new site at New Farm Loch in 1977.

DEAN STREET — Maisonettes (cottages on top of each other) in Dean Street, one of many attractive housing types provided under the Housing Acts after the 1939-45 war by the local authority.

PRIVATE HOUSING — Near the Henderson Church, in what was once the grounds of Braehead House.

THE DICK INSTITUTE, 1989 — The audio section of the modern reference library in the Dick Institute. Records, cassettes and compact discs are all available from the carousels. Whether music for pleasure, cassettes for learning foreign languages or talking books — they are all available from the library.

REFERENCE LIBRARY — This view of the reference library shows some of the hundreds of books available for consultation by the public. In addition to the books, information is also held on microfiche and also available, under staff supervision, from British Telecom's Prestel information service.

DEAN CASTLE — Records suggest that Dean Castle dates from the 11th century. Destroyed by fire in 1735, the castle and lands were purchased by the De Walden family about the turn of the present century. The Eighth Baron De Walden, with the help of the original plans of the building, restored the castle which, along with valuable collections of medieval armour and musical instruments, was gifted to Kilmarnock by his son in 1974.

THE VISITORS CENTRE — Today the lands of the Dean Castle serve the community as the Dean Castle Country Park. The Visitors Centre, to the left of the castle, functions as an information office with staff and exhibits to help visitors enjoy the park and nature trail to the full.

KILMARNOCK CENTRE — Taken from Portland Street looking towards King Street, the Kilmarnock Centre's main feature is the Burns Shopping Mall. Photographs earlier in this book show shops such as Scarletts and streets such as Duke Street which had stood on this sight.

BURNS SHOPPING MALL — Kilmarnock's first covered shopping mall opened in 1976 by Mrs William Ross. The Mall can be entered directly from the bus station and contains a wide range of shops, allowing shoppers to go about their business in comfort no matter the weather.

THE FOREGATE — Viewed from the new town centre, the Foregate follows approximately the line of Fore Street, which was demolished during redevelopment.

SQUARE OF ALÈS — Standing at the northern end of The Foregate, it was so named to mark the twinning of Kilmarnock with the French town of Alès. Kilmarnock is also twinned with Kulmbach in West Germany, Herstal in Belgium and Sukhumi in Russia.

TAXI RANK — Licensed taxis queue for hire outside the Mall in Kilmarnock Centre. Up to 1980 or thereabouts, anyone wanting a taxi in Kilmarnock had either to call at, or phone, a private taxi office. From 1981 when Kilmarnock and Loudoun District Council introduced a licensing scheme, taxis have been able to pick up fares in the street, and at designated ranks such as the one at the Mall. The District's first taxi licence was granted to Mr. John Struthers in 1981. Today, over 100 licensed taxis pick up over 7,000 fares a week. Radio contact with headquarters means that a taxi can be with a caller in little more than five minutes. In addition to giving normal door-to-door service, taxis are meeting an increased demand from women for carrying home the shopping.

WESTERN S.M.T. — A 71-seater Daimler Fleetline, typical of the elegant buses operated today by Western Scottish.

VIEW FROM THE PALACE THEATRE — The view shows the new bus station, multi-storey and open-air car parks. The railway viaduct in the background housed a variety of businesses under its arches until they were cleared out during redevelopment in the 1970s.

VIEW FROM MULT-STOREY — Looking over the modern bus station, from the multi-storey car park, towards the Palace Theatre and Grand Hall. The Kilmarnock Burgh crest is visible a little below the clock face on the Albert Tower.

THE NEW CROSS — The Royal Bank looks at ease in the presence of the new shopping centre.

OPEN-AIR MARKET — The market is established on the site of the old S.M.T. bus station which stood in Portland Street and was demolished in 1979 to make way for redevelopment. Successor to the Strand 'Barras', of the 1920s and 30s, the market operates in the town with approval of the District Council.

CORPORATION HOUSES —
Appropriately dubbed the pyramid houses, give Bonnyton a look of ultra-modernity. Built in the 1970s, they were specifically designed to house single people and the elderly.

D.H.S.S. —
Offices of the Department of Health and Social Security in Grange Street.

PORTLAND ROAD — Many of the properties in and around Kilmarnock town centre, originally built as houses, have been transformed into business premises. The view above looking towards John Finnie Street shows clear evidence of the transition from residential accommodation to commercial use. The sandstone cottage below has made attractive offices for a firm of solicitors.

CONVERSION INTO FLATS — A modern trend in Kilmarnock and throughout the country is the transformation of old large properties into flats. This villa in Portland Road is a fine example of this trend. The flats built behind are evidence of another modern trait, that of building homes for sale rather than rent.

PRESERVATION — A fine example of what can be done to modernise an old building in order that it serves as useful a function today as in the past. Once Borland's seed store 'The Artful Dodger' public house gives a touch of Victoriana to St. Marnock Place. The four iron wall lamps, on the face of the building heighten the effect.

CLYDESDALE BANK — The new Clydesdale Bank building, at the top of The Foregate. The upper storey features office accommodation for rental and is reached by way of the cylindrical staircase on the left. Kilmarnock Venture, started in 1984 to help attract industry to the area, occupies some of the office space.

A MODERN CHURCH — Howard-St. Andrew's, a striking example of a modern church. Built in the 1970s, it is located at the start of Portland Road some 50 yards from John Finnie Street.

ROYAL BANK — This ultra-modern branch of the Royal Bank, opened in 1975, seems to have already established a happy relationship with adjacent 19th-century architecture in John Finnie Street. Successor to two branches which started business in King Street after 1820, the new branch is one of three main branches of the Royal Bank now operating in the town. The second one at the Cross, a well known landmark because of its copper dome, was opened in 1939 to replace the 1855 original. The third branch is located at Riccarton.

TECHNICAL EDUCATION — Kilmarnock College in Holehouse Road has a lang pedigree as an institution specialising in technical education. The Science and Art School, built under the 1872 Education Act was succeeded in the early years of the present century by the Technical School in Elmbank Street, an adjunct of Kilmarnock Academy. About 1955, technical education was provided for a short time in Glencairn Primary School. That same year, students were transferred to a Further Education Centre housed in a building in Soulis Street which had begun life as a model lodging-house. Eleven years later, Kilmarnock Technical College was opened in Holehouse Road. Today, the 'Tech' is known simply as Kilmarnock College, reflecting its present day involvement in community education. It has over 3,000 students on full-time, block and day-realease courses, covering subjects such as engineering, business studies, hair-dressing, community care, arts and crafts, languages, catering, electronics etc.

THE MARTIAL ARTS — Kilmarnock can boast a variety of martial art clubs, covering a wide range of disciplines, including, Judo, Aikido, Kung Fu, Taekwondo and Karate. Karate has brought Kilmarnock particular success at competition level, producing; Pat McKay, World Champion in 1982 and 1984; David Coulter, European Champion 1978 and 1983 and Tom Gibson, European Champion 1988. Pat McKay and David Coulter have both been members of British Karate Teams which have won World Team titles. Pictured above are Tom Gibson (left) and Michael Coulter (British Lightweight Champion) of the Sakai Karate Club. David Coulter and his cousin Michael have a stranglehold on the Scottish Lightweight Championship David having won it from 1980 to 1983 and Michael every year since.

CLUARANKWAI — Eddie Cassidy of Kilmarnock's Cluarankwai Judo Club was five times Scottish champion, three times British champion and held the European championship before retiring from competition in 1972. Eddie gained his third and fourth dan (master grades) while studying in Japan and practising judo at Kodokan, Tokyo. Eddie, who still practises and teaches at the club, gained his 6th dan in 1984. The Cluarankwai was founded by Ted Routley in the 1950s and was the first martial arts club in Kilmarnock. It's name is a combination of Gaelic and Japanese and means "The way of the thistle". The Sakai Karate Club mentioned above was founded by John Kerr who was originally a member of Cluarankwai.

K.R.F.C. 1st XV, 1975-76 — Introduction of the Scottish Rugby League in 1973 saw the start of a long run of success for Kilmarnock. In 1974, the team won the Third Division Championship and were promoted to the Second Division. Finishing runners-up in the Second Division in 1975 gave them a place among the elite of the First Division. Season 1976/77 proved to be Kilmarnock's best season. They finished third from the top and had the satisfaction of seeing one of the team, Bill Cuthbertson, chosen to play for Scotland. Since gaining a place in the First Division in 1976, Kilmarnock have found it difficult to remain there. They are currently in the Second Division.

Standing (L to R): I.R. Cameron, D.D. Martin, W.G. Jamieson, I. Robb, D.R. Gibson, H. Hamilton, C.G. Alston, W. Mair, R.P.T. Muir. Seated (L to R): R.B. Campbell, E.L. Harris, H.R. McHardy, J.W. McHarg (Captain), R.D.A. Willock (President), W.B.N. Rose, R.H. Allan, J. Gibson. In Front: H.A. Smith, B.L. Mercer. Inset: J.F. Smith, D. Guthrie.

ANDREW ROSS — In 1924, Andrew Ross became the first Kilmarnock player to be capped for Scotland. Following this game against Wales he was capped on two further occassions.

BILL CUTHBERTSON — First capped for Scotland in 1976/77, Bill Cuthbertson has, to date, played 20 times for the national team and is the most capped player to have played for Kilmarnock.

CORPORATION BATHS — Pupils of St. Joseph's Academy on a visit to the swimming pool at the Corporation Baths. Opened in 1940, the Baths featured a wave-making machine, gifted by the Glenfield. Slipper baths for personal use were also available to the public.

THE GALLEON CENTRE — Use of the term Galleon, with its romantic swashbuckling associations, hides the Centre's true ancestry. It owes its name, in fact, to the Gallion Burn, a stream which originates beyond Grassyards Road and meanders for most of it's course underground before emptying into the Kilmarnock Water at the Douglas-street bridge. The stream itself was so named in honour of a lean and hardy breed of packhorse, the Gallion, which used to be common in Scotland and popular in the Kilmarnock area. The District Council's disregard of history, in naming the new recreation centre was a deliberate rejection of history, but a happy and justifiable one.

SWIMMING — Opened in 1986 on the site of the old Saxone Shoe Company premises, the ultra-modern Galleon features this swimming pool, kiddies' pool and flume. Tables and chairs provide the family-touch, so much the aim of the Galleon management. Besides the ice-rink seen in the picture below, the Galleon provides, among other activities, football, badminton, squash, gymastics, aerobics, weight-lifting and a sporting-injuries clinic. Instruction is also given in the martial arts.

CURLING — No need nowadays to wait for winter before being able to enjoy curling. Here we see one of five rinks in play in the controlled and comfortable atmosphere of the Galleon. The rink is also available for skating and ice discos, and may be used for ice hockey.

JOHN FINNIE STREET — Looking as elegant today as it was when building was completed in the last century. The foresight of the original planners in creating such a wide thorough-fare has meant that John Finnie Street copes well with a volume of traffic impossible to forsee all those years ago. Named after Kilmarnock-born John Finnie, who put up the money for construction of the street, its great architectural beauty makes it a fitting monument to his memory.